*"A true leader leaves a legacy and legacies
don't happen by chance.
So be proactive in your leadership
Inclusive in your planning and
Reflective in your execution.
As astronomical business growth happens
when we invest in building excellent teams"*

— Melanie Folkes-Mayers

TABLE OF CONTENTS

CHAPTER EIGHTH

CHAPTER NINE

CHAPTER TEN

CHAPTER ELEVEN

DEDICATION

To my beautiful, smart and cheeky daughters Eden and Zahara, without the blessings of you coming into my life this book would not have been possible.

You gave me the impetus to create my legacy to the world so that you could see that anything is possible if you put your mind to it.

Always remember life is too short to leave things to tomorrow, take action and enjoy the journey.

INTRODUCTION

"Do what you love and you'll never work a day in your life"
— *Confucius*

Are you running your business like a boss but your team aren't catching your vision and executing it the way you need them to?

Is managing a team (even a team of 1!) taking up way too much of your time, patience and energy?

Or

Are you ready to build a team but you are scared that you'll mess it up and end with more drama rather than less work to do?

Sheila was desperate to have a team member to help in her shop, serving customers and dealing with the online orders while she created her amazing cakes and deserts (who knew that you had to get chocolate to the perfect temperature to make chocolate bonbons?), but she'd never managed staff before and was concerned about employing someone and how to make sure that she didn't end up stuck with an employee that she couldn't work alongside.

I worked with Shelia to not only find the ideal candidate but to develop the practical leadership and management skills that she needed to feel confident to employ her amazing assistant, that she now can't live without.

This book is designed to support you in becoming the best leader and manager that you can be on a practical level. Teaching you how to set the standard, coach and mentor, develop and empower in your own unique way so that you get the very best out of your team WITHOUT having to micromanage.

I wrote this book because years of working corporately revealed that the main reason for staff issues was a lack of effective staff management. This was mainly due to a lack of management training, which led to both staff and their managers being frustrated, plus due to inconsistencies in how employees were managed, motivated and developed grievances were being raised.

Too often people who are excellent in their roles are promoted to leadership positions without any coaching, mentoring or formal training. Being a great team player doesn't mean that someone will be a competent team leader.

Leaving the management of the team responsible for the growth of your business to chance is too big a risk to take.

Whether you already manage a team or are thinking about moving from being a solopreneur to an employer, you need to read this book and take the actions described to make sure that you are a proactive leader who:

- Demonstrates the leadership behaviours and qualities that you want to develop in your team
- Recruits the best candidates
- Engages well with your team
- Empowers your team to take ownership
- Trusts their team to deliver excellence

Most business owners and entrepreneurs that I speak with start their business as a passion project; they are great at creating a product or delivering a specific service and have subsequently decided to step out and supply those in need of their skills. But we all know that a business can only grow so far as a one-man/woman enterprise and, at a crucial point, you will need to become an employer, manager and leader of a team (whether it's for one or one hundred people).

The Performance of your team will be the difference between the success and failure of your business, invest in building your leadership and management skills so that you can be proactive rather than reactive in your interactions.

Managing a team effectively is a skill that we all have to work to develop. Recruiting, developing and managing a team is rarely a "love" for anyone, which is why most CEOs employ an Operations Manager as soon as they can afford one. However, that can be a long time coming and may not be the best investment for your business, as with the right team of effective managers in place, you can delegate to gain the freedom you need to focus on working within your zone of genius, without that extra layer of management.

We start the book by looking at you as a leader, identifying your needs and aspirations beyond your business. Understanding what success looks like for you, helping you to be clear about what you need from your business and team.

We look at how you take care of yourself and get the help and support you need to take care of your mental health and deal with any stressors.

We look at how you manage your tasks and how you ask for help and delegate.

Then we look in detail at the behaviours that you and your team should develop and demonstrate to ensure that you build a culture that is empowering, inclusive and productive.

The answers to your leadership and management challenges are all here with practical implementation tips, you just have to put in the work.

PREFACE

"When your why is big enough you will find your how."
— *Zig ziglar*

If you are wondering why am I the right candidate to write this book and share my views, tips, and strategies with you or maybe you are doubting and asking, will they even really work? Let me just share with you that I have been where you are; Having lived the experience I know that the reality of leading and managing a team is far removed from the theory that I read in books and learnt at university.

Let me give you an insight into what that looked like...

My HR career advanced quickly, mainly due to the fact that I loved a challenge and never said 'no' when an opportunity came knocking. So, it wasn't much of a surprise when I found myself managing a local government department of 67 people, when previously I'd only managed teams of four or five.

It was a totally different ball game, going from managing staff that I had recruited, developed, and knew intimately, to a department that was established and wary of the changes that being outsourced can bring. Also, while I was childless and in my early thirties, all of my direct reports were older with grown or teenage children and their priorities were different to mine. They were not motivated by progression and status but stability and flexibility.

When I look back now, I cannot help but think, I must have seemed so naive to them, full of energy to push through change, but with none of the background knowledge I needed to make it happen. I visualised the fancy new systems that I needed to implement, but I hadn't prepared for the journey. My staff were already overworked, with a backlog to clear and managers were complaining about delays, while all I was doing was adding to their workload without showing them the benefits to come.

> *"When your why is big enough you will find your how."*
>
> Zig ziglar

My team was frustrated and so was I, which meant I fell back to my normal pattern of just working harder and longer hours to get everything done myself. It didn't take long to realise that it wasn't sustainable when running a whole department and I needed a different solution.

I started to think about how I would advise a manager if they were having difficulty motivating their staff, and I realised that I'd fallen at the first hurdle. I hadn't engaged my team or asked for their knowledge and advice as we made plans and moved forward.

Consequently, I pressed reset and spent time with each of my direct reports to get a clear understanding of their roles and responsibilities and where their struggles were. Then I discussed my ideas for new HR systems and processes and how they could improve our service and reputation with the business. My team were excited with the concept and helped me to make it better, but they still had a backlog to get through; so I requested in some additional funding to hire some temporary staff to clear the backlog. This provided support to enable my team to become more involved in the project to ensure it would function the way we needed it to.

It meant a slight delay but the project came in on budget and painlessly, most importantly we were able to implement a system that worked for my team and our clients and is still in place today.

Change is a constant in any business. It is important that you can lead and manage your team to grow your business astronomically, even in times of uncertainty, and this book will give you the keys to do so.

I have always loved solving problems and helping others. As a child I spent most of my time curled up in the window of my bedroom lost in a book. I loved imagining myself as a member of The Famous Five, or some other Enid Blyton book.

I was an only child for the first nine years of my life. I lived with my mum and grandmother who was a loving, caring, no-nonsense Christian lady, who gave up her job and became a childminder when I was 3 months old so that she could take care of me while my mother worked. The house was filled with children from 7 am to 6 pm, but I still preferred my own company - a good book was all I needed.

At primary school, they let me loose in the local library as I was reading above the levels they had. I would devour books, completing them in one sitting. Time stood still. I wouldn't hear my mum or grandmother calling me for dinner or to do my chores – something I would get into trouble for. And still do!

I had a very strict upbringing, I was really only allowed to go to church events, there was no playing out for me. I only learnt to ice skate because it was a class at school and my boyfriend (now husband) teased me terribly when he discovered that I was 25 years old and had never learnt to ride a bike. We planned a trip to Center Parcs and I had to enrol on a crash course so that I could get around. I learnt to ride a bike in my 6-year-old goddaughter – how embarrassing is that?

One of the positives of being raised alongside the church was that there was always something to get involved in. I attended Saturday school, learnt to be hospitable to visitors and make sure people had what they needed, I babysat, learnt how to touch type and coordinate others, and I got to sing and speak in front of hundreds of people. I loved to help out in any capacity and was often asked to train others.

What didn't go down so well at church was the fact that I wanted to understand how things worked and why we do things the way we do. If I didn't get a reasonable reason for why I had to do/not do something, I simply stopped (or started) doing it; therefore I didn't understand why I couldn't wear jewellery or makeup, so I wore them, despite the tellings off, and now everyone is wearing them!

I cannot blindly follow, I need to make an informed decision. I need the background to understand why I am completing a task or not allowed to do something. This is probably why HR is my chosen field. Most issues can be resolved by understanding the context, the individuals involved, and the legislative constraints. I always start with the outcome I want and then work backwards to make sure that I am starting from the position that will give me the very best chance of drama-free success. It's like playing chess, you work out the strategy before you start and adjust as the game progresses.

I am a combination of a read/write and kinaesthetic learner. I learnt to drive a car by first reading a book about how the engine, three pedals and gear stick worked, and then when I got into my driving instructor's car I tried out the theory practically.

The ability to put theory into practice is why my first career choice was IT. I studied Computer Science as an undergraduate and became disheartened by the fact that I couldn't get involved in the final solution part of the project, just the coding. So when I left university, rather than join an IT consultancy and sit coding in the basement, I got a job with an international publication that needed an office manager who could create and maintain their content database. I loved it. It was great to have the responsibility for creating the solution and amending it as needed.

As it turned out this is also the role in which I found my HR calling. Human Resources also became my responsibility and, as I did my background research and completed a foundation course, I realised that HR was the link between the people and the technology, and that was the element I most enjoyed.

Once I realised that HR was my swim lane I never looked back. I've had the opportunity to work strategically and operationally in roles with local, national and international remits. I've worked in retail, IT and strategy consulting, education, local as well as national government and charities for nearly 20 years.

One thing I've found to be fundamentally true is that building or developing an effective, efficient, growing business requires proactive action from the top down. It does not happen by chance. Each business decision that you make must be taken with the holistic view of your customers and your team.

This book was nearly called Leading with Love, because treating your team and your customers the way you would like to be treated, even when giving challenging feedback, news or direction, is essential to getting your team to deliver excellence, even in challenging times.

Once I had to close an entire office in Scotland, and at the end of the process, the staff gave me hugs. The service didn't slip and they contributed to ensuring the work was handed over to our other offices because they were committed to the business and its clients.

I've also had to make two people, out of a team of 40, redundant and they caused as much disruption to the team and the reputation of the business as they could.

The identifiable difference was the forethought and the preparation, taking time to proactively look at the individuals affected and communicating with care and consideration.

If I could leave one lesson for the leaders and managers in the world it would be to be PROACTIVE; take time to plan and prepare your steps before you take action. It may add a little time to your journey, but you'll get there with fewer bumps in the road.

CHAPTER ONE

MANAGING YOURSELF

"Time is equal to life; therefore, waste your time and waste your life, or master your time and master your life."
— *Alan Lakein*

How are you managing?

Managing and leading others is a lot about setting the right example by demonstrating the behaviours and work ethic you'd like your team to develop and maintain.

So before we start to look at managing others well, let's establish the skills and behaviours that we need to develop in ourselves and demonstrate to others, as we empower them to support us, as we build and scale our businesses.

We can't expect our team to epitomise our businesses values if we aren't doing that ourselves. It's like telling your children that lying is bad and then telling them to answer the phone and say you aren't there. You'd be giving mixed signals and allowing for grey areas, where there should be none.

Whether you believe it or not you are a leader, people are watching everything that you do and emulating what they see, so it's vital that you set the right example by demonstrating the behaviours you want your followers to adopt, to get them to truly believe in your cause and follow you.

You will always need to work with others, even if you are aren't directly employing and/or managing them, so you must develop the skills to help you to do so, without it taking up a bunch of time and tearing you away from sharing the amazing skills, talents and knowledge that you have and the world needs.

One of the biggest lessons I learnt when working corporately was that if I was struggling to get everything done, either I didn't have the skills needed to deliver, or I was trying to do too much. It's a lesson I've had to remind myself over and over again.

The first few months of starting my business, I had so much work on, I just focused on delivering quality to my clients and enjoying the increased income, but when those projects came to a close I realised that I hadn't taken the time to build a pipeline or cultivate relationships with other potential clients.

I'd invested time and money in developing my HR skills and knowledge but not in all the other things that it takes to run a business like; content creation, networking, social media and advertising. And that is a lot!

I wasn't managing myself effectively. I knew what I should be doing but I didn't do it because I had tunnel vision and I felt like it had to be all or nothing. I would pull all-nighters trying to tick off all of the things on my to-do list and be grumpy and short-tempered for the next day.

I was all in when it came to delivering excellence for my customers, but I wasn't when it came to making sure my business was set up properly for success. I had to work smarter not harder, play to my strengths and make time to rest.

I needed to remember why I started the business in the first place.

I started my business to support business owners in proactively building their teams and business, I wanted interesting and challenging work and I wanted to spend more time with my young family.

What is your why?

I had to learn to keep my why in mind when I set my objectives, made decisions on what to work on and most importantly what not to work on.

It was pointless accepting all of the work that came my way if it wasn't in my zone of genius because it wasn't taking the business in the direction that it needed to be headed.

I had to learn to introduce my clients to others in my network who could deliver what they needed, without worrying about not taking that income myself.

I couldn't also accept working with clients that weren't aligned to my values as I wasn't prepared to sacrifice my integrity.

> *"Not all money is good money."*
> — *Unknown*

At the same time, I couldn't accept all the work that was on offer because I needed to prioritise balancing time with my children, as they were a big part of the reason I decided to move away from corporate employment to business ownership.

Knowing and being able to articulate what I wanted was the beginning of building the team I needed to support my team and business growth.

What do you want?

> *"Start with the End in Mind."*
> — *Stephen Covey*

First things first, you cannot go on a journey without knowing the destination at the outset. In life and in business, you need to know where

"Not all money is good money."

Unknown

you are headed and be able to articulate it clearly to others. That way it will make it easier to know which opportunities to say yes or no to.

I am not talking about having a detailed business plan here, although they are very useful (and I'll look at setting objectives for your business and team in a later chapter). I am talking about knowing what you would like to achieve personally and then creating the steps to do so.

For example, my client Pauline runs a successful childcare company across multiple sites. She was ready to scale her business to offer additional services to the hardworking stressed parents that use her services, but she was so busy running her business that she couldn't see how she could find the time to do anything else.

While we were working on building capacity within her business, it was vital to build the business in a way that gave Pauline the balance and income that she needed, without burnout.

With that in mind, one of the first things that I asked her to do was to complete the table in Figure 1 to focus her thinking.

"Start with the End in Mind."

Stephen Covey

The table requires you to write in your short, medium and long term goals for your Faith, Business, Health, Relationships and Money. Short term is 4-6 weeks, medium-term 6 months and long term 12 months.

Faith is all about how you centre yourself and bring the best of you into every situation, your goal could be about regular prayer, meditation, reading, journaling, etc.

Business relates to your business aspirations, that could be an income, profit, number of clients, speaking engagements, employees, etc.

Money can relate to earnings, savings targets or investments.

Health relates to how to maintain your physical health, that could be anything from eating healthily and doing some regular exercise, to not working over the weekend.

Relationships looks at the people in your life; parents, siblings, partner, children, friends. What activities would you like to do with them and how frequently?

Fun is all about you and what activities light you up. It could be a trip to the cinema, holiday in Thailand or a pedicure every month.

I would suggest that you complete this for yourself as all of the areas interlink. E.g. If you put a figure in the **Money** column for what you'd like to take home, that will correlate to how much income you need to make in your **Business**. Likewise, the Fun elements will influence how much free time you need.

Your objectives need to be clearly defined. I like to use the SMART framework, Specific, Measurable, Achievable, Realistic and Time-bound. So instead of writing, 'spend more time with my family', put 'spend at least two hours of uninterrupted family time each week, with no technology'.

You should be able to put steps into place to achieve these goals, and they should stretch you a little, as the saying goes.

> *"Shoot for the moon. Even if you miss, you'll land among the stars."*
> — *Norman Vincent.*

When Pauline completed the table, she could clearly see her destination; she wanted to free up some time to work on new business projects, grow her business, spend time with her family and work fewer hours. Now, all we needed to do was create a plan to help her get there and then execute that plan.

Take some time now to complete the table for yourself and then we can move on to the next brick in the foundation.

Areas	Short Term 4 – 6 Weeks	Medium Term 3 – 6 Months	Long Term 12 Months
Faith	Reading positive podcasts		
Business	income insta shop		
Money	earn a wage. £500		
Health	Food week walk to work. yoga home.		
Relationships	9 - once a week friend once a week		
Fun	clothing 1 x month Baking fancy		

Figure 1.

You can only really focus on achieving three to five objectives at one time, and while many of the objectives that you've detailed in the chart above will interrelate, you'll need to prioritise and once you are on the way to achieving those objectives, move on to the next one on the list.

This is why setting realistic short and medium-term goals is the key to giving you the momentum needed to achieve your long-term objectives.

Now that you know what your personal objectives are you can then break them down into manageable tasks and schedule them, so that you don't miss any vital steps which prevent you from achieving them.

Get rid of the rush

It's impossible to successfully build and scale a business without some organisational skills; and while many leaders say organisation isn't their strength and have the good sense to get someone in to keep them on task and time, that is only possible once a business is established enough to bear the cost of administrative support. Even then you'll still need to be able to communicate what you need as you hand the tasks over.

So what do you do in the meantime?

I have been called the Time Management Queen, but I really put it all down to being organised. I'm able to stick to deadlines because I keep organised, I know what is needed and when, and I am prepared to prioritise my workload accordingly.

Do you struggle to keep all the business and life plates spinning?

There are individuals who love the adrenaline of working to a tight deadline, always running from one emergency to another. NOT ME! I am not a person who is great at working down to the last minute of the deadline. Seeing the clock ticking makes me panic, my brain gets fuzzy and I lose focus. I basically want to give up, because the perfectionist in me knows the outcome won't be perfect if I'm rushed, so I just don't want to do it at all!

There was a time in my life where I would have chosen to go back home rather than arrive at an event late!

So, for me being organised is essential to function as a person, let alone to be a Great Manager. To manage well, I need to be on top of things so that when the inevitable drama comes around the corner, I can be prepared.

If there is one thing that I can guarantee, it is that just when I have a deadline, there will also be a client emergency and maybe a sick child to console, or school project to complete that sucks up my allocated last-minute polishing time and why I have a poster that says **'Done is better than perfect'** on the wall in my office.

Last year I spent the week before Christmas working from my dining room table, while my eldest daughter was stretched out on the sofa with chickenpox! If I didn't already have Christmas planned and my work scheduled I would have been in trouble. Instead I arranged for childcare for my external meetings and was able to deliver most of my work from home between my nursing duties.

Though different from a sick child, lots of distractions can occur during your working days, especially once you add staff to the mix. Have you ever had a day (or series of them!) where you were busy from morning to night but you can't for the life of you remember what you did? It's so easy for your to-do list to never get touched while you react to all the issues that arise.

To keep my life organised I use several tools, some digital, some old school!

For home life, I have a monthly planner in the kitchen that has a column for each member of my family and a column for meals and events. This means that I am not thinking about what to cook, where we need to be or whose birthday is next; a little time to prepare at the beginning of every week is all I need.

For the business, I use a weekly planner in Excel that has all of my scheduled tasks and meetings, as well as any deliverables that I need to work on that week. It is printed out and attached to the whiteboard above my desk to keep me focused. It is also used so that I can visually see if I have any gaps in my schedule to accommodate additional work, rest or play. There is an example below:

Time	Monday	Tuesday	Wednesday
6 am	Run	Gym	Run
7 am	Shake/Shower Girls up and Breakfast	Gym	
8 am	Dressed / School Run	Shower	
9 am	Check Emails		
10 am			

I also use a digital calendar that has all of my meetings scheduled and use Asana for project planning.

How I start my day is generally an indication of how it will work out, so I am very intentional with how I start it.

How do you start your day?

I am a person of faith so I start my days with prayer and exercise, but I remember that when I first started running, I would either start late or shut the front door behind me in a rush to meet my running buddy, only to discover that I'd left something vital at home. It tended to be my running watch, which I needed so that I could assess my speed, distance, heart rate, etc or my earphones so that I could listen to some motivating music or podcast. Delaying getting out of the door would be down to me searching for my trainers, favourite running socks or some other item of clothing needed due to the AMAZINGLY changeable British weather.

You see I'm not great in the morning, I'm basically asleep with eyes open for the first thirty mins, so basic recalls of memory can fail me.

I needed to get organised, so I prepped the night before.

I checked the weather before going to bed.

I started laying out absolutely everything I needed the night before; shoes, socks, running bra, running gear, running pouch, running watch and earphones, wet or cold weather garments when needed.

This means now I get up, put the kettle on, get dressed, have some hot water with lemon and I'm good to go.

I'm no longer scrambling in the dark, trying not to wake up my husband as I search for my running gear at 05:30 in the morning or rolling over in bed making excuses for why I'll run tomorrow instead.

However, being organised isn't just about making sure that you are prepared for the task and have all you need close to hand. It also requires you to be mentally prepared to do the work, because with all the preparation in the world, I do sometimes go out and five minutes in I find that I want to turn around and go back home.

Fitness instructors often talk about muscle memory. That it takes a while for you to get the hang of a technique, but once you've got it, it becomes second nature, so that even if you have a few months off, you can get right back to it. I guess it's like that saying:

"You never forget how to ride a bike."

Even once I'd gotten out of my house with all of my running gear, I needed to know what to do and where to go. I found out that it's not just one foot after the other, I needed to warm up, so I wouldn't be in agony for days after. I had to find a pace that was steady enough to maintain, yet challenging, and I needed a route that would be clear but safe at 5:30 in the morning. So, I researched dynamic stretching, ran with an awesome friend who knew the best routes and through practice learnt how to go at my own pace.

It was hard, but the first time I ran 5K without stopping it felt awesome and it gave me the incentive I needed to keep going – that was 5 years ago. Now I run regularly and should I miss a run or two, my muscles gently remind me! My trainers should have their own passport, I take them everywhere I go!

All of that organisation has meant I've been far more consistent in my running which has paid off in fitness and mental health gains, as well as providing a regular early morning slot with my creative self!

Being organised as a manager or leader means that you don't just look the part, but you do the work and keep working towards your goals.

This means that those around you KNOW that they can trust that you will do what you promised. Nothing is more frustrating for a team member than not knowing where they stand. I once had a manager who constantly postponed meetings or promised to do things, that then wouldn't get done on time or at all.

It meant that I lost trust and felt like I was abandoned and had no support. Ultimately it was part of the reason why I left the company.

An organised manager or leader also sets a great example. Even if you aren't purposely stating that you are organised, those around you will observe the way you work and how you get things done. I never had to tell my teams that I expected them to leave their desks clear at the end of the day, or that they needed to come prepared to meetings, they observed how I worked and did the same.

If you are not naturally organised – I have some pointers to help you get organised and stay that way.

- Work out the morning routine that sets you up for the day and make sure it happens.
- Plan ahead, write a to-do list at the end of each day so that you'll know where to start in the morning.
- Have dates for completing your tasks and use them to help you to prioritise your to-do list.
- Focus on three tasks for each day, that way you can guarantee you'll complete them and if you have more time, you can go to the next task on the list.
- Work in 25-minute slots so that you can keep focused and don't get overwhelmed.
- Keep track of actions that you need to take after meetings or calls so that you don't miss anything.
- Set calendar or telephone reminders if you need a reminder.
- Take regular breaks and don't forget to eat.

Being organised and managing your time well will always be a challenge for you as a business owner. It's easy to get caught up working on your own passion project, it's why I'm up writing this book after midnight when I should be in bed.

Nobody is perfect! I say this to myself as well as you, you will burn out if you don't balance your time effectively and where would your business be without you?

You haven't finished building your legacy yet.

Where does your help come from?

"Closed mouths don't get fed."
— *Shabazz Muhammad*

Do you find it easy or hard to ask for help or support?

When you have a business challenge is your first thought, 'How can I fix it?' or 'Who can help me fix it?'

I'll bet you generally go into the solve-it mode, I used to do that too…and being totally transparent sometimes I still do!

As an entrepreneur, it can be difficult to release the reins and allow others to work on your 'business baby'. You've put in so much into building up your business you want everything to be perfect.

Both in my corporate and entrepreneurial life, I have struggled with delegating the time consuming administrative and technical tasks to others, as I was SURE they couldn't do it as well and/or as quickly as me, and if I was going have to teach them and then check it afterwards, I may as well have done it myself!

But I wasn't doing myself any favours, I was busy being busy, my business wasn't growing as quickly as it should have been because I was trying to do ALL THE THINGS, and my team wasn't learning or developing. Which meant that I was in a constant cycle of pitching for work, overwork and stress, complaining that there was no one to help me. However, the situation was of my own making.

I needed to delegate the more time-consuming administrative and skilled tasks to my team and trust them to be great in their area of genius so that I could be great in mine.

The whole idea of recruiting and building a team is to free you up to do the high-value stuff, like speaking with potential clients and delivering excellence to your paying clients, it should also mean that you can go on holiday WITHOUT your laptop, iPad and iPhone, take the afternoon off to relax in the spa, or go to your children's school play without worrying about what's happening in the office. After all, you became an entrepreneur to have freedom and flexibility, not to be connected to technology 24 hours of the day.

I've had many clients say they are so busy they need help, but they have no time to find someone, or they just can't find someone who they can trust to do things just how they want it done! Fact is, it doesn't matter how it's done if the end result is what you want and no compliance regulations are broken.

When I've broken down the reason why most business owners lack trust in their team, it's because they fear they'll get things wrong, that they'll change the winning formula that has gotten them this far.

Fear is a strong emotion and has its place. Fear can literally save your life, but running a business is about taking calculated risks and mastering your fear, the definition of **Entrepreneur** is:

'A person who sets up a business or businesses, taking on financial risks in the hope of profit'

I'm not asking you to just hand over your work to just anybody and hope they'll deliver. You need to build a team of qualified, competent individuals who have the skills and behaviours that you need to scale your business and accelerate its growth. Then with the right framework in place, you need to release your team to be great, so that your business can grow.

Like my client, Alice, who was struggling to focus on building her business because she was caught up trying to get the day-to-day things completed. Her company mobile phone would not stop ringing, as her managers referred any difficult customers to her rather than dealing with them themselves. This meant that the majority of her customers had her number and would just call, rather than talk to the manager for the relevant store (even though they'd be seeing them face to face regularly). The head office line hardly rang, so Alice's assistant wasn't inundated with calls. Alice felt trapped.

After spending some time with Alice it became apparent that her caring and maternal nature had meant that her managers didn't even attempt to solve tricky problems, they just called Alice for the answer. My first suggestion was to change her mobile number and remove it from all the business literature. Each store and store manager had a telephone number and there was a number for head office too. Alice struggled with the idea until I reminded her that she was the boss and didn't need to be held hostage by her business, she had to take care of the situation or it wouldn't change.

We delivered our signature management training programme to the managers and their deputies, created a peer coaching group and created a crib sheet for the managers to be sure they understood the policies and processes so that they took ownership for managing issues and didn't need to disrupt Alice, except for emergencies. A month after the phone was disconnected Alice said

"I feel like a weight has been lifted, I don't know why I didn't do that sooner, thank you"

Change is hard, even if it will make life easier for you in the long run, so many talented leaders struggle with letting go and getting the help their business needs to accelerate to the next level. So with this in mind, here are a few signs that it's time to start delegating:

- Its 3 pm, you've been working all day, but haven't completed any of the MUST DO tasks on your list
- You've just spent the last 3 hours trying to make ONE SIMPLE CHANGE to your website
- You can't remember the last time you switched off your laptop before 10 pm
- You can't remember the last time you had a no technology day (email/mobile/Facebook/Twitter/Instagram)
- Some days you get to the end of the day, have been ridiculously busy but can't name a thing you've done and so have no sense of accomplishment
- Your only solution (regularly) is to just work through the night, so you can get everything done

If this is you, it's time to consider what tasks you can delegate and then train, coach and mentor your team or find a service that you can outsource some tasks to.

My business is my baby and unlike my children, it doesn't verbalise the desire to be free of my clutches and so I sometimes struggle to hand things over but then complain about a lack of time. Delegating is always a major subject in our Management and Leadership coaching programmes, so I thought I'd share a few tips to help you find those extra four hours in the day:

Play to your strengths

Know what you are good at and stick to it. When you started your business you were a team of one and had to get everything done (sales, products, accounts, marketing, logistics). Now you can buy in support, either though outsourced providers (accountants, VA, social media, contractors) or employees. Get the right support in and give them the autonomy to deliver.

Getting support doesn't mean that you have to lock yourself into a full-time permanent contract. If you are concerned that your business might experience a downturn (or you know the support you need is seasonal), you can hire casual staff or offer a contract on a fixed-term and/or part-time basis.

My client, Phil, knew he had too much work for at least six months and was concerned about the time investment that it would take to train someone up for one project. We got really specific about his need and found a candidate with all the skills he needed who wanted to work part-time around their caring responsibilities, and who was happy for a six month trial after being off of work for two years. It was a perfect match. Phil was no longer overworked and his new team member was doing the work that they loved in a way that matched their own needs.

Don't overthink the challenge of finding your ideal candidate, trust me they are there, you just have to look in the right place.

Take the time to train your team

Have you ever said, "By the time I teach them how to do it, I could have done it myself!" Ten years ago this would have definitely been me, but by the time I'd had to complete that task three or four times, I was wishing that I had trained someone, ANYONE else in my team to do it.

As annoying as it sounds, you have to invest time to free up time, whether it is setting up a system, process, or training an individual and this is the same thing I say to clients who are too busy to find time the hire the staff they need – it's chicken and egg! A fully trained and empowered employee means more freedom for you.

Albert is an amazing carpenter who can conceptualise an idea, take measurements and build something without a drawn plan. It's all in his head, which is fantastic but makes others working with him more than frustrated, as they can only move forward with a project with him around. He drops tasks like breadcrumbs and his team follow until they run out. Albert was frustrated because he couldn't get a break, even if he was sick he needed to be on site, otherwise his team wouldn't be as productive.

Albert found it difficult to share his vision, so when a new project started, instead of going to measure up and discuss the options with the customer on his own I suggested he should take a member of his team and have them take the measurements to create the first draft and then sit with the team to discuss the plan and get everyone to input. It took a couple of attempts but the outcome was amazing. Albert and his team discussed the plan and made changes, the changes were added to the plan (not by Albert) and everyone knew what was happening. This meant that projects were completed sooner and that projects could run concurrently, which meant more satisfied customers, less work for Albert and increased business.

It's impossible to accelerate your business alone, you have to develop trust in your team so that they can add the extra bandwidth and skills you need to make your business soar.

Invest the time in making sure that your team is fully trained and that there are training manuals in place to help them, should they miss a step in the process. And do not feel that you have to create that process. Train your team and have them document the process and keep it up to date, then whenever you have a new joiner or promote a team member you have a process manual ready!

Not to mention you should have a process manual for disaster recovery purposes! Please tell me you have? And if you don't that should be at the top of the To-Do list for someone within your organisation.

Block out your time

It is really easy to get distracted by the admin needed to run a business even with an administrator or VA on staff, so block your time for specific tasks.

When I worked corporately, I had a colleague whose calendar was always full. I wondered how she ever got any work done and then I realised that she scheduled her work into her calendar, colour-coded, with alerts to ensure that all her work got completed on time.

I'm not that organised but I do write down my Must-Dos for each day and the time that I am dedicating to them. Then at the allocated time I close down my emails and put my phone on airplane mode so that I keep focused. Does anyone else have a mother that always calls when they are on a deadline?

I use a variation of the Pomodoro method. Instead of working for 25-minute sprints with a 5-minute break, I work for an hour or 90 minutes and then take a longer break. This helps me to focus on a particular project as I find that it can take a while to get into the zone and once I get there it can be difficult to stop (and I like to complete tasks in one hit if I can).

Unless there is an emergency (or holiday) I try to only do my admin tasks on Fridays so that I don't get distracted. I schedule in time to meet with my team, write content, call clients, connect with social media and support my clients. This means that my team know when I'm available and I know what I need to achieve during the day.

To get this book written, I committed to 2 hours of writing 5 days a week, I scheduled it in first thing in the morning, but if a client emergency came up, I made sure to move it and refused to go to sleep until I'd put my hours in, it was the only way that it would have been completed. I knew if I didn't schedule the time, and stick to it, I'd be dreaming of being an author instead of actually becoming one.

If there is a project that has been on your wish list for a while and you keep saying "I don't have the time", block out the time, be ruthless and stick to it – even if you have to act as though you are headed out to a meeting to get it done. Which takes me to my next point.

"The graveyard is the richest place on earth, because it is here that you will find all the hopes and dreams that were never fulfilled, the books that were never written, the songs that were never sung, the inventions that were never shared, the cures that were never discovered, all because someone was too afraid to take that first step, keep with the problem, or determined to carry out their dream."

— Les Brown

Change your location

When I first started my business, I worked from home and would spend the first couple of hours in the day, cleaning and tidying before I started working and then would be carrying out other chores too. Have you ever popped into the supermarket to come out two hours later?

It didn't take long to realise that being at home wasn't helping my focus and so I found a co-working space to work from. The change of location was just what I needed, there were no dirty dishes or laundry to distract me but lots of businesses to connect with.

Once you have a team (working alongside you or remotely) it can be easy to be constantly distracted with their tasks and challenges. I used to struggle when I overheard a conversation that I wanted to chip in on; my ears would switch on and the focus on my task would go flying out of the window.

And, because my team knew that I wanted to share, they would ask me for my opinion on every challenge. There were definitely opportunities to coach, but I wasn't allowing my team to use what I was teaching.

I needed to move out of their sight for my team's sake as well as mine. If you are constantly being interrupted by your team asking for your help (for outcomes that they are capable of delivering) or you can't resist 'offering' assistance and keeping all the real decision making for yourself, it's time for you to find somewhere else to work from at least one day a week, to give you and your team some space to be great.

Firstly, make sure that they have that process manual that I spoke about earlier in place, so they can find the answer to their problem and then you can go to a place where you can focus. Some of my clients work from home a day or two a week so that they can work uninterrupted, others go to a local hotel lobby or make a day of it and go to work from a nice hotel in central London.

I have a few local coffee shops, pubs and restaurants that I can escape to. I put my phone on airplane mode, connect to the wifi and I find I can get a day's work completed in half the time when I have no interruptions. I'm on a train for 3 hours tomorrow and I already have a work plan.

You have to give your team the skills they need to succeed and then trust them to deliver in your absence: this can be hard especially if you tend to hover and offer unsolicited advice and direction. However, micromanaging your staff isn't healthy for you, your team or your business. None of you will be working to your full potential.

I have a client who was going into her office for a few hours most weekends so that she could get some work completed uninterrupted as her open-plan office is always bustling with managers popping in to speak with her team. One day we had our regular catch-up meeting in her office rather than at the local coffee shop and I could see her being distracted by all of the comings and goings, wanting to listen in to conversations and check out what her team were getting up to; all-in-all I could see that more progress would have happened if she'd stayed out of the office, so I suggested she worked from home one day a week and discover if that eliminated her need to come into the office over the weekend. A month later she told me how much she was able to achieve on her dedicated day out of the office. She got her weekend back and was happy with the way her team performed in her absence. Win-win.

The saying that, what you don't know can't hurt you, was definitely true in this circumstance. If there is truly an emergency your team will get in touch, don't worry it will be fine.

Are you self aware?

"Many leadership problems are driven by low self-awareness."
— *Bill Hybels*

Back when I ran a recruitment team, it was standard practice to ask candidates about their strengths and weaknesses. Often savvy candidates would try to transform a positive into a negative like, "I'm very detailed so I can struggle to do a quick and dirty job, I prefer to put in the time to make sure it's perfect" or "I'll always pitch in to help my team, even if it means taking on more work".

And I totally understand why they would do that, I'd probably do that myself. No one ever got the job by saying, "I'm really last minute but I get it done, I thrive on the adrenalin".

However, the questions about strengths and weaknesses are really about finding out how self-aware you are, and as a business owner and leader, it is imperative that you develop your self-awareness and that you encourage your team members to do so too.

Self-awareness will save you and your team a lifetime of frustration.

Have you ever asked a member of your team how they thought their work was going, to have them give you the standard "fine" response, when you know things are not fine? It makes the lead into that difficult conversation just a little harder.

Admitting that there is a problem will make it easier to find a solution, but naturally, we try to protect ourselves from pain, and pride will have us struggling on our own. I remember getting frustrated trying to stretch my daily 1440 minutes to be all things; CEO, wife, mother, daughter, friend, and not asking for help because I thought I needed to do it all myself. Believing that asking for help was a sign of weakness.

But, I have rarely asked for help and not received it, because if someone asks me for help I will do all that I can to assist them.

Being conscious of our own strengths and weaknesses is one thing, but being open enough to share that with others without fearing judgement is a different thing altogether. You need to create a safe space that allows your team to be honest with you and that starts with you being honest with them.

I had a CEO ask me to get them an executive assistant that would keep them in line and make sure that they got to where they needed to be on time, with all of the right documentation, because they weren't good at that kind of thing. Being transparent about her weaknesses meant that I could be really specific with the job description and, when I did the first round of interviews, all shrinking violets were eliminated. The successful candidate not only had the skills that were needed, but, also had the temperament and behaviours that were needed to be successful in the role. Additionally, as I got to share her with the CEO I gained more support than I would have asked for, but she made my life easier too.

"Self-awareness is one of the rarest of human commodities. I don't mean self-consciousness where you're limiting and evaluating yourself. I mean being aware of your own patterns."

— *Tony Robbins*

When you know what you aren't naturally good at, you can either spend more time developing that skill, by taking a course, getting someone to review the task for you and giving you feedback, or you could choose to delegate it. My husband is excellent at processes mapping, data and analytics, but can struggle to explain things clearly and concisely, so he asks me to sense check his communications as explaining complex things simply is one of my strengths.

On the other hand, I know that I can be easily distracted by an idea, I can end up going down a rabbit hole researching something really interesting, but not relevant to the task in hand, has that ever happened to you?

There is often value in the idea or the conversation, but I need to keep on top of my tasks, so because I know that I can do that, I assign timings to tasks and have others keep me honest. But I do also write down or voice note the idea and, when I have time to pursue it, I go for it.

The same applies to assigning tasks to my team. I'm good at using Microsoft Excel, but I don't use it every day, so I always need to refresh myself for the more complex formulae and macros. Some of my team, on the other hand, use Excel every day, so it makes no sense for me to waste time on a task that they can do quicker than me.

I always advise my clients to either outsource, recruit or develop the skills that they are missing/find challenging within their team; we can believe that we need to be able to do everything ourselves (and we should understand how everything works). However, what we should be doing is perfecting our skills within our zone of genius so that we can provide our mastery to those who need it.

"Great leaders are not the best at everything. They find people who are best at different things and get them all on the same team."

— *Elieen Bistrisky*

Do you know what your strengths and weaknesses are? And that of your team?

As part of your annual/biannual review process, you should be assessing the skills of your team and yourself, comparing those to the skills that you need to achieve your business goals, now, or as part of your 1, 3 or 5 year plan, and then address any gaps.

This could be training, recruiting, outsourcing, partnering or acquiring another business with those skills; isn't that what Mark Zuckerberg does? Acquire the competition or create a better version?

If you have a team, a great way to assess their skills is to complete a 360 degree review; taking feedback from the individual, their peers, subordinates, clients and stakeholders will give you a holistic appraisal of their strengths and weaknesses. It should give you the evidence you need to assess any skills gaps and have an objective conversation that drives improvement and development.

If you don't have a team at all right now but want to build one, the most straightforward way to assess what skills you need in your team is to detail all of the tasks that you do over a couple of weeks. Write a list of all the tasks you do and how long each task takes.

For each task decide if you are going to keep or delegate them. The tasks you keep should be those things that you are uniquely qualified to do and those that bring income into your business.

Task	Time Taken	Keep	Delegate

Now that you have a keep/delegate pile, sort the tasks into groups - admin, social media, data analysis, accounting, etc. This is how you will start to put a statement of work or job description together.

You may have to complete some tasks you want to delegate because they are vital to the success of your business and you aren't able to delegate or outsource them immediately, but as you grow you can see what work you should delegate or outsource first.

Are you coachable?

When was the last time you read a book, attended a conference, took a course or worked with a coach or mentor?

And then have you taken what you learnt and actioned it?

There is a lot of information out there, it's never been so easy to access information, but it doesn't do a thing for you if you aren't actioning it.

When I was completing my master's degree in Human Resource Management I had the choice between studying as a distance course, or attending 2-3 classes a week at a London University. I was working full time and the distance course looked like the easier option from the outside, but I knew that I needed the accountability of classes otherwise I'd end up leaving my studies to the last minute and prioritising my work commitments. There were days when I left my office and worked from my phone until I stepped into the classroom when I had to stop, but if I had been headed home to study, I would have just stayed in the office solving the issue.

It can be like that in our business, we know that we need to invest in building our skills, but the demands of the business take priority and the things we prioritise are the things that get done.

To get this book written I had to get myself a book coach, she had to remind me to schedule my writing time otherwise this book would have never been completed. There is always a fire to put out when you work in HR, but I needed to remember that my client's emergencies aren't my emergencies – I can be timely and still complete my business generation tasks.

The most successful leaders seek knowledge and action what they have learnt so that they keep progressing. Learning comes in many forms; you can take a course, read a book, listen to a podcast, attend seminars, have a mentor, invest in a coach, even just having a chat with someone can improve the way that you approach your life and business.

Finding time to up level your skills while you are building your business can seem impossible. It can be easy to get stuck doing things in the same way, especially when you are running your own business. You are fantastic, you know what you are doing and you know what your clients need, but that will change over time and if you don't continuously learn you'll be left behind.

> *"If we rest, we rust. So keep moving."*
> — *Darius Foroux*

You have to be open to innovation; to take input from your team and clients and put a plan into place to deliver. If you have the right team with the right skills, or the ability to develop them, you may not have to deliver the changes yourself. Simply work with your team to develop the idea and then allow them to run with it.

I worked in the IT industry for a significant part of my career but the coding that I learnt at university is no longer used. The machinery and software that we use now I couldn't have even imagined then. I have friends that I studied with who have kept their skills current and those who stuck with their preferred systems. Guess who is in demand and commanding the greater salary? Those with the up to date skills. If I tried to get back into coding now it would be like starting from scratch.

In HR the regulations are updated regularly and the outcomes of cases and appeals at tribunal can affect the interpretation of those regulations, so it means that I have to keep up to date with the legislation to be able to support my clients. If I didn't, I could get my clients into more trouble instead of out of it!

However, I don't have to keep up with the different ways that businesses find new clients, provide services, do their accounts, etc. I have to make a conscious effort to do that for the good of my business, to ensure that I leave a long-lasting legacy of HR excellence.

Most recently I completed a Mental Health First Aid course, it was an investment of time and resource but I could see that the need to provide our clients with sound mental health advice for both themselves and their team was increasing daily.

What unanswered need do your clients have that you could deliver?

CB had been running a charitable organisation for years, delivering excellent youth intervention services and delivering it all with mainly a team of volunteers. She came to me saying that she needed to employ two individuals to run some programmes that she had received funding for. I asked her for all of the details so that I could use the correct contracts and, when I reminded her of her obligations as an employer to provide a pension scheme and contribute to it, she was shocked. She hadn't realised that the legislation had changed and so hadn't budgeted for it as part of her staff costs. Now that is why she came to me, but, had she just dug up the old contracts that she had previously used and issued those, she would have been in breach of legislation and at risk of reputational damage – something that no charity (or any organisation) wants to experience. We changed things around and decided that a contractor's contract was a better option, as the roles were linked to funding received for a relatively short period, was not full time, plus both individuals were happy to register as self-employed and deal with their tax obligations.

We have to be coachable to be able to stay current, but also to learn from our mistakes and fall forwards, otherwise the same mistake can be made over and over again.

Like the local restaurant who kept getting orders wrong and, when complaints were made, they didn't apologise as a first response but rather defended their position. At first, the locals forgave the errors as teething problems and continued to eat in and order deliveries, but after a while, when the orders were still incorrect, the complaints increased and so did the prices, at which point the locals stopped going there to eat. The business was not profitable and the restaurant ended up closing.

There were so many things that the restaurant could have learnt and changed to build a loyal following of locals who would have paid the increased price for delicious, fresh, local food (and the food was tasty!), had the service and orders been up to scratch. The feedback was freely given (on social media) but the owners did not address it.

Being a business owner can be lonely, the buck stops with you. Which means you are bearing the weight of your business and all of the challenges that it brings. You must have a safe space to share and download.

Finding a tribe or someone you can trust with your business dream, bounce ideas with and complain about the challenges can be hard. If your family or friends aren't entrepreneurially minded they might not understand your challenges and get bored with the conversation.

Also, to be fair it can be annoying having to explain yourself all the time. Especially when what you really want is someone to say, "I've been there and this is what worked for me", or "Let me introduce you to blah blah. Who should be able to help".

Finding a business coach that you can work with on a one-to-one basis or as part of a group coaching programme will give you support, accountability and help you to accelerate your business quicker. There's no better thing than to learn how to avoid the mistakes that others have made, and instead of trawling the internet for the answers, having them delivered to you in a structured format that you can refer to and action immediately.

I was a year into running my business full time before I realised that I needed to invest in a coach that would help to accelerate the growth of my business. The investment hasn't always been financial. I've been part of sponsored growth accelerators and had mentors to pour their knowledge into me, but when it has come to specific needs, I have invested and seen a return on my investment before I'd even completed the course – obviously I needed to take action, and act on, what I'd been taught. Those lessons have stayed with me and I refer to them often.

So tell me, how are you staying coachable?

Are you taking care of yourself?

*"Rest and self-care are so important. When you take time
to replenish your spirit it allows you to serve others from
overflow. You cannot serve from an empty vessel."*
— *Eleanor Brown*

Do you know the signs for when you need to take some time out and rest?

There is a lot of talk about self-care but often it is looked at as a manicure or spa day, rather than a daily investment in your mental health.

Being mentally healthy is key to being effective in all areas of your life. Personally, if I am not taking care of myself properly, I get snappy and the whole atmosphere in my home changes.

I completed a Mental Health First Aid course to help me support my team and stressed out clients (little did I know that it would highlight some changes that I needed to make too!). Two things really confirmed the importance of good mental health:

1. The Stress Container
2. Your Stress Signature

Think about your stress container as a funnel with a tap at the end. All of the things that can cause you stress flow into the container.

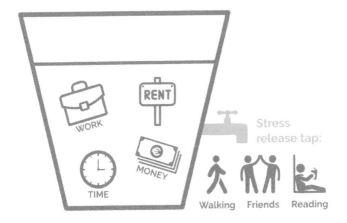

You stressors could be; work, children, family responsibilities, financial concerns, health concerns, worries for the future, etc.

The size of the stress container varies from person to person and can change over time. So some people may be able to deal with a great deal of stress, while others may only need a little amount of stress to feel overwhelmed and unable to cope.

The tap demonstrates how you are able to relieve the stress, there are positive and negative ways to release that stress:

Positive Stress Release	Negative Stress Relief
Talking to a friend	Drinking alcohol
Exercise	Recreational drugs
Journaling	Staying up all night
Meditation	Binge eating
Bubble bath	

You should try to release your stress before your stress container becomes full. You should become aware of the fact that your stress container is full (or getting there) by your stress signature.

Your stress signature are the signs that you are getting stressed, for me I experience stomach issues and my skin breaks out. I have difficulty switching off so my sleep is disturbed and I get snappy.

When I did the Mental Health First Aid course, I realised that I would stay up all night to get the work that was stressing me completed, as a way to release the stress, but it would leave me wrecked for the next day.

Now, when I start noticing the signs of my stress signature, I get an early night, get up early for my run and then attack whatever task or issue was. I find that with rest and a clear head I can deal with anything.

Can you identify what your stress signature is? Ask those closest to you. My husband was able to identify my stress signature better than I was.

I have spoken in the earlier chapters about organisation, time management, delegation and self-awareness, all of these things are elements of self-care in my eyes.

We need to make life easier for ourselves; taking on too much, trying to do things in too little time, and trying to do everything ourselves does not serve us.

To give the very best to those around us, we have to be at our best. That means taking care of ourselves first, just like when you are on an aeroplane and they tell you to put your oxygen mask on before you help others.

Make sure that you have what you need to be successful and then help your team to have the same.

Serving others from a place of lack will lead to resentment and you can't serve gracefully when you resent it. The resentment will show in your delivery.

Early in my business, I had a client who needed some assistance recruiting some staff and after I completed that task, she told me that she was having a problem with her website, and so I showed her my set up and suggested she do the same. She wasn't very tech-savvy so I ended up doing it for her, but after I handed it over, she kept coming back to me asking for additions. Now I'd assisted as a favour, and websites aren't my area of expertise (or a part of my business at all), and I began to resent the constant questions and queries. Every time I saw her number flash up on my phone I would become agitated. In the end, I directed her to someone else and distanced myself from her.

I would have been better off if I'd directed her to someone else to assist her rather than trying to do it myself.

We must stay true to ourselves, keep our why and our zone of genius at the forefront of all we do and allow our team to do the same. It's ok to say no to things that don't take you in the right direction.

A very wise woman once said to me "You don't win any prizes by being the first to arrive and the last to leave. Either you aren't up to the job or you have taken on too much and aren't asking for help."

Ask for help, lean on your team, take your rest and keep your focus. You'll be a great leader that others will want to follow.

"Talk to yourself like you would to someone you love."
— *Brene Brown*

CHAPTER TWO

MANAGEMENT BEHAVIOURS

Now that we've covered what you need to do to set yourself up to demonstrate the right example as a proactive leader, we are going to delve into the essential behaviours that you and your team should be demonstrating every day.

The first thing that I must say is recruiting the right candidate is the key to building a high performing, proactive team. Recruitment is a process that requires an investment in time for planning and preparation. You have to know what you want from a candidate before you finalise the job description, advert, interview questions and scoring matrix.

You can access our FREE HR Knowledge hub with lots of tips and checklist for a smooth recruitment process here http://bit.ly/HRKHub

I always advise my clients to recruit more for behaviour than for skill, you can teach skill but it is very difficult to change behaviour – Not impossible, but very difficult. If you find a candidate that has 70% of the skills and 100% of the behaviours, I'd recruit them over someone who with a 100% skills match with 80% of the behaviours.

The selection criteria for any role should not only include the skills that you need but also the behaviours. You should be getting evidence of how a candidate works and why they work that way. For that reason, I often ask candidates to complete a case study and/or deliver a presentation as part of the selection process. It allows me to see how structured a person is, what steps they would take and why.

The way a person behaves often based on their experience and what has worked (or not worked) previously. We had a client who had a member of their sales team that was an excellent salesperson but a terrible team player. His focus was on getting the sale and making his commission no matter what. He would over-promise to the client, which would mean that the delivery team had a hard time getting everything done on time and he wouldn't share his sales skills with junior members of the team.

There had never been expectations set around appropriate behaviour, which made managing him difficult, as far as the salesperson was concerned he was exceeding his sales targets, what else was there to do? He didn't know that the delivery managers hated working on projects that he had sold as he never checked that what he was agreeing with the client was possible within the allocated timeline.

The salesperson had worked in sales all of their life, in competitive industries where you were only as good as your last sale. They had moved to an industry where the sales process was more complex and it was important to build a long-lasting relationship to ensure that the customer was a happy repeat customer, who referred the company to others.

My client changed three things to reinforce the behaviour that they wanted to see:

- Added behaviours to their objectives and performance review process, so that they were the gate openers for bonuses (the percentage of bonus you received was aligned to meeting behavioural expectations). Eg. If you haven't completed your sales paperwork on the system, you will not be eligible for a bonus.
- Customer satisfaction and repeat orders were added to all salesperson job descriptions so that the 'sell and run' method of sales was eliminated.
- A representative of the delivery team was included as part of the sales process to ensure that the agreed solution could be realistically delivered.

You should have a set of behaviours as part of your business mission, vision and values package and all of four of these elements should be communicated to your whole team, your team should know them as they should be the golden thread that runs through your business.

But just in case you don't have any, let's just be clear about what these four elements are before we move forward:

I like to describe the **Mission and Vision** as the departure and destination. Your mission should be what you aim to deliver to your clients as a day to day standard, whilst your vision is where you aspire to be.

So for my business, our mission is:

'To provide the HR expertise that you need to confidently recruit, manage, motivate and develop your team so that your business can achieve astronomical growth'.

Our vision is:

'To be the top-ranked HR consultancy for SME's in the UK'

Values are what your business stands for; that could be Sustainability, Courage, Innovation, etc. They are what you tell the world your business is about.

For Eden Mayers HR Consulting our values are *Dedication, Focus, Knowledge and Efficiency.*

We have a values statement that we share with our clients and team, it is:

We are **Dedicated** and **Focused** on helping businesses and individual's progress positively.

We are **Knowledgeable** about our business, experts in all areas of HR, data analysis and project management.

We are **Efficient**, we can work quickly and help you get the results you need.

Creating a values statement is an easy and memorable way to communicate your values to both your team and customers. Even if you are a solopreneur at the moment you should still create a values statement to share with your clients (and be prepared for your team once you have one).

The behaviours that you expect from your team are unique to the type of business you run and what is important to your clients. A vegan restaurant will have different behaviours set than a luxury car hire company. I have listed some examples below:

- **Ambitious:** strongly wants to succeed
- **Conscientious:** taking time to do things right
- **Creative:** someone who can make up things easily or think of new things
- **Curious:** always wanting to know things
- **Logical:** using clear and sound reasoning
- **Organised:** dealing with one's affairs efficiently
- **Precise:** careful and with great attention to detail
- **Altruistic:** shows selfless concern for others
- **Caring:** desires to help people

- **Compassionate:** feels or shows sympathy or concern for others
- **Considerate:** thinks of others
- **Faithful:** being loyal
- **Impartial:** treats all persons equally; fair and just
- **Kind:** thoughtful, caring
- **Polite:** exhibiting good manners
- **Sincere:** being totally honest
- **Affable:** friendly, good-natured, and easy to talk to
- **Assertive:** confident and forceful
- **Authoritative:** commanding and self-confident; someone who is likely to be respected or obeyed
- **Charismatic:** shows a compelling charm that inspires devotion in others
- **Enthusiastic:** showing intense excitement, interest, or approval
- **Persuasive:** able to convince others to do or believe something
- **Self-assured:** confident in one's character

This list is not exhaustive, I will be discussing quite a few in the chapters to come that are not mentioned on this list. You should pick 3-5 core behaviours and then you could add a maximum of another three that may change according to roles and responsibilities.

For my business, the core three behaviours are *Curious, Resilient and Persuasive.* I picked these three because delivering a solution that is specifically tailored to each client definitely requires curiosity, building lasting relationships and getting CEO's and their teams change their ways of working requires persuasion and being able to deal with life's challenges well and keep pushing even when its hard is something that I believe every leader needs to develop.

These behaviours are not just for your leadership team, you should expect them to be demonstrated throughout your organisation and you should definitely use them as part of the performance review process.

Steve was so frustrated with the way his team dressed in the office, no matter how many times he said 'smart casual', people would turn up in jeans, trainers and unironed t-shirts. Even new additions to the team started coming into work smart, as he'd instructed during the recruitment process, but within a month their standards slipped too.

You didn't have to look far to see what the problem was, the CEO came into the office in flip flops and shorts, often covered in dog hair – the only way the team knew that an important meeting was taking place was when he showed up in a shirt and trousers, with his hair brushed!

Have you ever had this kind of experience?

Leading others effectively is impossible if you are not prepared to demonstrate the values and behaviours that you wish to see and develop in your team.

Say your values are: Transparency, Responsiveness and Innovation.

How are you embodying them daily?

Does your team know what your plan is for business growth?

Do they know there is a problem BEFORE you start reducing the outgoings?

Do you respond to requests for help or assistance promptly (even if it's just sending a holding message)?

Do you shoot down any ideas that don't come from you?

Do you think your team would be transparent, responsive and innovative with you, your business or your customers?

Being a true leader means taking a hard look at yourself and making the changes that you need to influence in the right way because whatever you do positive or negative you are making an impression on those around you.

Take this quick exercise and see what you need to work on:

- Take a pen and paper
- Write down your top 3 – 5 core values
- Write down an example of how you have demonstrated (or not) each in the last 2 weeks

Be honest, if you can see that you aren't demonstrating your core values, make a plan for how you can set a better example for your team.

"Leaders Bring You Along, Managers Push You Along", have you ever heard that saying?

There are distinct differences between a manager and a leader, even though you do have leaders who manage and managers who are leaders.

As a business owner you are already a leader, even if you don't think so!

Remember when you started your business? You had to motivate yourself, push forward and make things happen. You had to win that business, make the sale and convince your family, friends and funders that your business was a going concern and that will be hugely successful.

You led them to understand your business, to join you on your business journey as a client, investor or cheerleader. That's what a leader is, someone who takes people with them on their journey, using a compelling message.

Sounds easy right?

As an entrepreneur, you need to have the skills of both a leader and a manager. It's not easy as often influencing others to take the right path can take more time than just directing them to a task! And time is always short for an entrepreneur!

However, the pluses for leading your team is that by giving them greater autonomy, you get freed up to do the high-value tasks that only you have the skills to deliver and who knows what amazing ideas your team may have for improving your business, creating efficiencies and increasing your bottom line.

Often when I work with business owners who are strapped for time, I encourage them to delegate entire projects to members of their team so that they can dip in and out of the strategy and get the project completed without it taking up all of their precious time. I was talking to one of my clients last week who was blown away by the quality of work delivered by one of the junior members of her team, but she would have never delegated that piece of work had she not been time poor. The will be gems in your team but if you don't coach them for the next level, you may never find out about that diamond in your team.

Below are some of the differences in the behavioural characteristics of a leader and manager:

Manager v Leaders Behaviours

Manager	Leader
Drives employees	Coaches them
Depends on authority	On goodwill
Inspires Fear	Generates enthusiasm
Says "I"	Says "We"

Manager	Leader
Places blame for the problem	Fixes the problem
Knows how it is done	Shows how it's done
Uses people	Develops people
Takes credit	Give credit
Commands	Asks
Say "Go"	Says "Let's Go"

Think back to the last five conversations that you have had with members of your team, have you been communicating more as a leader or a manager?

There will always be times when you all need to be more direct about what your team needs to do and that isn't a problem if you have established a relationship so that your team are with you on the journey.

Even when it comes to my children and telling them to do something rather than asking I always give the rationale so it will be "Put your shoes on we're going to be late for the party" rather than just "Put your shoes on", I needed them to do the task but I am also giving them the reason to do it. I'm taking them on the journey with me.

The most effective leaders are authentic and keep it real with their teams. You can be yourself and be a successful leader, your team will connect best to your authenticity.

When I was promoted to my first big leadership role, I used to try and emulate the managers that I'd had a positive experience with in the past. I used to ask myself "What would Sue/Simon/Sophie do?". I'd try to embody them before I went into a room to have a difficult conversation but I realised over time that I wasn't able to properly connect with my team and stakeholders because I was using a script that I'd made up in my head.

Have you ever done that? Created a whole scenario in your head, where you've thought through all of the options, just like a game of chess? Maybe it is just me.

The script meant that I was speaking but not really listening, I was just waiting for an in so that I could say my next line. This meant that I never shared anything personal about myself and could remain professionally distant. Interestingly for me, I got pregnant just before beginning the role and as my pregnancy progressed, conversations with my team that started with shared tips on pregnancy and childbirth, slid into conversations about work-life balance, workload and client challenges, I was able to understand my team's pain points and motivational drivers and use them to share what I'd learnt delivering projects.

And while I still think through scenarios and try to be as prepared as I can be for any questions or issues that may arise, I've found that going into a meeting with an open mind and reading the room has made for far more positive outcomes.

It's the little things that make the connections that motivate your team. You should be able to tell if something is concerning your team member and if you make the right connection, they will tell you their issues (whether personal or private) if you ask.

Okay so let's move into talking about the specific behaviours that are vital for the success of your business as you lead your team after I tell you a little bit about Servant Leadership.

CHAPTER THREE

SERVANT LEADERSHIP

"To lead people, walk beside them…
As for the best leaders, the people do not notice their existence.
The next best, the people honour and praise.
The next, the people fear; and the next, the people hate…
When the best leader's work is done the people say,
We did it ourselves!"

— *Lao Tzu*

There are a lot of different leadership models and I'm not going to get into them in detail, but I do want to talk about my favourite.

Servant leadership is, in my opinion, the very best type of leadership. It's really about understanding that you are a facilitator for your team, that you don't have to stand on a podium to capture hearts and minds, but instead that provide your team with what they need to be successful. I call it leading with love.

The best leadership experience that I had during my corporate career was at an organisation who ensured that everyone within the company knew the mission and vision of the business and how their objectives aligned to them. Then we were all given clear instructions and the feedback, training, mentoring and coaching to be successful.

I ran the graduate recruitment programme for them and ninety-five percent of the graduates recruited stayed with the organisation for over three years and progressed by at least 2 levels. The graduate programme was better than I've seen run at multinational organisations. Everything possible was put in place to guarantee success. Every new starter was given a buddy to support them in getting acclimatised as soon as possible and a mentor to help steer them as they developed their careers. Our graduates were out at client meetings and giving their opinions within the first two or three weeks. Consistent positive and constructive feedback was given, during my time there we only terminated two contracts and both were individuals who were not a values match.

This organisation thrived because the entire leadership team were servant leaders, every manager mentored at least two junior members of staff, regular detailed feedback was given and any training needs were addressed. There was an understanding that nobody is perfect and that learning could be messy. There was a focus building a high-performance culture while ensuring that the team had a good work-life balance so that they could perform at their best.

The biggest lesson that I learnt while working here was that if I was feeling overworked, I needed to speak up and get help to make it manageable, whether that was training for me or additional resource. There was a recognition that working long hours continually was not healthy and would not enhance my creativity or progression within the organisation.

Even years later at the reunion party, the graduates that I recruited, who are now married with children and specialists in their field spoke with fondness of their time with the business and many of us have worked together again as our careers have progressed.

I was really lucky that one of my first corporate roles enabled me to see this method of management and development in practice. Servant leadership is a skill that I have taken with me, implemented and taught to others. It has never led me wrong.

A servant leader is focussed on bringing the very best out of their team by creating an environment that provides the elements necessary for success and then gets out of the way so that their team can excel.

Of course, it's not as easy as it sounds, we are all intrinsically selfish and put our needs above the needs of others. We need to shift from thinking about what others can do for us to what we can do together, which will be rewarding for all.

The other challenge is moving away from a blame culture, rather than wanting to find the person to blame for a mistake or omission we really ought to be focused on solving the problem and agreeing the mechanisms to prevent that mistake happening again.

At the heart of servant leadership realising that having a successful business is the environment that you create.

Being a servant leader is providing your team with what they need to be successful, opening doors, providing training, coaching and developing individuals to excel in their zone of genius. But often leaders can be more of a hindrance to progress rather than a help.

As a leader and business owner, you can be the gatekeeper for a lot of tasks within your organisation, which is fine if you can respond promptly to every request, but the truth is that if your business is growing and you are stretched, then your team will struggle to get hold of you and so delays will happen.

Once I accompanied a client to a meeting with a software provider, my client already used the software but wanted to be licenced to provide it as a solution to their customers and provide an outsourced managed service option as a separate offering.

We sat with five members of their team in a large boardroom set in a beautiful stately home, surrounded by acres of grounds with a very fancy coffee machine and was told that the Founder and CEO lived in one wing with his family while the business was run from the other wing.

We had a very thorough demonstration of the product and a tasty lunch but every time we tried to negotiate a point or see if an element could be added, someone had to go and check with the CEO. It was an arduous process and in the end, my client chose to go with one of their competitor's products, delays can cost you business.

Your team are your businesses representatives, how you treat them and support them is how they will treat your customers.

As important as it is to get feedback from your customers, it is just as important to get insight from your team on what they need and how they are feeling. This can be a quarterly survey (and its always great to capture the statistics to compare) but having an environment where your staff are comfortable to share concerns and challenges when they occur is more important. Your team needs to see you addressing their concerns, this might not be making the changes that they are requesting but at the very least taking time to review and give the rationale for why changes cannot be made.

Maslow's Hierarchy of Needs (1943) is a motivational theory that looks at the five elements that an individual needs to be fully fulfilled.

Figure 3 - Maslow's Hierarchy of Needs

Each of the levels builds on each other, starting with physiological needs moving up through to self-actualisation, with the needs lower down in the pyramid needing to be satisfied before those higher up can be attained.

Physiological and safety needs are described as basic needs, while love and belonging and Esteem are described as Psychological needs. The ability to satisfy these four needs are a motivating factor in themselves and the longer an individual is without them, the stronger the desire to attain them becomes.

It is easy to see how many of these needs can be provided by having a stable job, consistent income, job satisfaction, appreciation and a relationship with peers and management. All of the things that a servant leader would be providing to their team as the basic standard.

However, once the first four needs are met, they are no longer a major motivating factor, as the individual seeks to attain self-actualisation. Self-actualisation could conceivably be unending as there can always be a higher height to achieve.

At this stage job enhancement, promotion and career development opportunities are important, as otherwise, your team will look for their next growth opportunity with another organisation or perhaps start their own business.

On average we spend more time working than any other activity per week, except for sleeping. Its important that the work environment is positive, not just a place to come to get a salary. For a lot of people, their sense of self comes from their job and the appreciation and sense of accomplishment that it gives them, this can be especially true for those who may live alone or have a home that is not a haven.

A few years ago I supported a company that wanted to pilot having their Customer Services Team work from home; some employees jumped at the chance to avoid the commute and work in their PJ's but others refused to try, I remember one guy telling me that he rarely spoke to or saw anyone he knew from leaving work on Friday to coming back into the office on a Monday. He took two busses to get into the office and had a 2-hour commute but he'd prefer that to being stuck at home all of the time.

He wasn't the only one, out of 120 employees only sixty percent were interested in working from home permanently, and a further 20% said that they would only be prepared to work from home for 2-3 days per week. There were a raft of reasons, from a lack of privacy, young children in the home to not having space to accommodate a desk, chair and files.

It is important to remember that every member of staff will have a different list of things that motivate them and it will change over time, they will be covered by Maslow's theory but how you provide it and manage them will vary. The important thing to remember is that your team are individuals and their needs will change, so you need to keep having an open dialogue to keep the surprises to a minimum.

As a servant leader, it is important to create an inclusive, open, supportive culture and maintain it by setting the right example and dealing with any behaviour that doesn't align to values and behaviours that you have identified for your business.

Not taking action is an action, you are demonstrating that its ok not to meet the expectations that are set and your sanctions become meaningless.

If I tell my daughter that I'll bring her back some chocolate when I could home, she'll have an expectation that I will return home with the chocolate, if I don't bring it she will be disappointed and if I do that several times she will lose faith in me.

If she misbehaves and I say that I will take the chocolate away if she continues that behaviour but when she misbehaves I do not take the chocolate away, she will have no reason to adjust her behaviour.

The same applies to your team, you build trust by doing what you have promised and you lose respect by not doing what you promised or following through on the sanctions (policies and processes) that you put in place to address non-compliance.

To be a servant leader remember:

- That the success of your business is not all about you
- To provide/source the resources that your team need to be successful
- To be clear on the mission, vision, values and objectives
- To demonstrate the values and behaviours you want your team to emulate
- To treat your team as if they were your customers
- To be collaborative
- To work with your team

- To address any behaviour that you do not like as soon as possible
- To show your appreciation

CHAPTER FOUR

TAKING OWNERSHIP

"To think about your life is to create it. You have to take ownership of where you are right now and know where you want to go before you can get there. Keep collecting evidence for your success. You can believe it, and you can be it."
— *Ali Vincent*

One of the positives of being an employee is that is for the majority of people there is always someone senior who can take the slack or fix a problem.

When I worked corporately, I could go on annual leave without worrying about my team or my clients, I could always delegate to someone and not worry about what happened in my absence until I returned. I was very clear that my corporate laptop and mobile phone would not be accompanying me and that I expected only to be called for a genuine emergency.

And to be fair the only time that I was called, was when a member of staff got seriously hurt in another country and I needed to rally the insurance company to repatriate him.

When I was a new business owner for a long while that wasn't true. I didn't have someone the fall back on, the buck started and stopped with me and while I don't regret the holidays where my laptop accompanied me and paying for the WIFI upgrade was a business necessity, I'm glad that I no longer need to do that.

My default has always been to try and do ALL.THE. THINGS. and then I get exhausted and begin to resent having to do everything, and complain that no one is helping, but the truth is I didn't ask and if you don't ask you won't get.

I do it at home all of the time. When lockdown started in March 2020, I went into fix-it mode. In fact even before it was official and I realised that I couldn't get my usual supermarket delivery slots (I hate queuing; supermarkets, banks, post offices) I took myself to the supermarket to get the essentials and made sure that we had everything that we needed at home. Then when my husband was sent home with his laptop and wide-screen monitor until further notice, I gave up my office corner so he would be comfortable and worked from the dining table while home-schooling the children. Then I got annoyed, everyone was loving being home but me, I couldn't get 5 minutes to myself; I was taking care of everyone else's needs but my own. Even though my office space was open, I was at home taking calls in the garden or car as it was the only place to get some peace and I was working after the girl's bedtime to keep up with my to-do list.

I'd failed to ask for help AGAIN. No one was offering to help because I had it all under control, in my mind it was my job to make sure that everyone was ok. But the moment I asked for help my husband and I split the schooling, so I did the morning shift and he took the afternoon and I started going back into my office once or twice a week (where a lot of other parent entrepreneurs were also hiding out!).

All it took was for me to release the need to do everything myself, ask for assistance and not get caught up with happened when I wasn't there. It might not have been done the way that I would have done it but everyone got fed, the children were educated, the house was clean and most importantly I wasn't exhausted and could be 'in the moment'. I wasn't thinking about work when I was with my family or feeling guilty about not dedicating enough time to homeschooling when I was working.

The first step to getting your team to take ownership is you releasing ownership and delegating the responsibility. There is a quote in the Bible that says *a dog cannot have two masters'* Matthew 6:24 and while it refers to deeper spiritual stuff, it is true that it is impossible to delegate to your team and still have everything done your way.

A big challenge for the majority of my clients (and myself) is that we want help but we want things to be done exactly the way that we would do it and if that is how we delegate tasks our team will never take ownership, the moment the process we have stipulated runs into an issue they will come back to us to resolve rather than use their initiative.

We need to be outcome focussed, that is to ensure that the outcome we desire happens; quality, timeliness, compliance but not how it happens. The destination over the journey.

I have a client who couldn't help 'assisting' the managers with his team. He would have a meeting with his leadership team and tell them to disseminate the message to their teams but then he would 'sit-in' on their team meetings to observe and then take over the conversation. It meant that his managers didn't take ownership of the message or dealing with members of their team who weren't adhering to any rules. My client would vent his frustrations that his team constantly came to him to fix their issues and say "they've seen me deal with issues, they should be able to do it", but when I asked about letting them lead the conversations he would say "I have to interrupt they don't do it the way I would, so I have to speak up".

The issues with having that attitude was that people only progress if they can be in a sticky situation and work their way out of it, it may not be elegant, but it will get better over time. No one is perfect and you have to be ok with that. Think about when you learnt to drive, were you the perfect driver the first time that you got behind the wheel? I know I wasn't. I remember that even when I was taking my driving test my instructor told me that I wasn't supposed to be perfect, I was supposed to be safe. It was only after I passed my test and was driving alone that I had to manage manoeuvres without assistance and develop my skills as a driver. The tiny places that I park my car in now, I would have never attempted when I first passed. Practice makes perfect.

To get your team to take ownership, you have to give them the responsibility to deliver and be prepared for them to fail. I know that sounds scary but I'm not suggesting that you start with asking your team to deliver to your biggest client with no support, but that you start to hand over tasks that you really ought not to be doing and build up to the big stuff.

If there is a problem be there to show your team how to fix it, but don't get drawn into trying to fix the issue yourself. These are teachable moments, sure it takes more of your time in the beginning, but it will feel fantastic when your team are fully trained and you are free to focus on the bigger tasks.

You need a team that you can trust to deliver well if they aren't you need to put your capability and conduct policies and procedures into action.

Also, remember that not giving your team the chance to stretch and develop is holding them back from their full potential and if your team feel that they are being held back, they will be demotivated as demonstrated by Maslow's theory that we discussed in earlier and they will leave when they find the opportunity to shine elsewhere.

And I've been there too...

"Does your daughter use proper cutlery at home?" my daughters preschool teacher pulled me aside to ask. "No, she has plastic cutlery". The teacher handed me a child-sized set of metal cutlery and said let her practice with these at home.

Oh, the shame!

I'd been holding back my daughter's development and I never even realised it! I'd love to tell you that this was the only time, but there have been other instances when my children have come home with new life skills that I hadn't realised they were ready to develop.

The same applies to your teams, getting your team to take on increased responsibility and ownership for the outcomes that you require means that you need to open up opportunities for your team members to develop like my client Alice who was struggling to focus on building her business because she was caught up trying to get the day to day things completed.

She had three team managers but was managing their teams herself, recruiting and doing performance reviews.

At first, I thought that the manager's job descriptions would need updating but all the things they were supposed to be doing were written in there, they'd just never been required to deliver. So, we updated the manager's objectives. delivered our signature Management Fundamentals course and implemented regular peer coaching sessions so that the managers could learn from each other.

Now Alice coaches her managers through staffing issues and empowers them to deal with issues themselves so that she can focus on providing additional products and services.

If you are struggling to get your team to take ownership, try the following:

1. Focus on the outcome rather than the method.
   Don't worry about how your team will deliver the desired outcome, give them the parameters (timelines, budget, legislative boundaries, etc) and let them deliver.

2. Ask questions rather than giving a solution.
   Aim to coach your team, ask them open questions to get them to think about the solution, learning how

to think out of the box and be creative is a skill that requires development.

3. Provide training to support.
    You can't expect your team to deliver if they don't have the skills to do so, provide the training that they need to deliver; that could be training from you or a colleague, an online or classroom-based course or a process manual.

4. Create process manuals (with your team) so their reference tool isn't you.
    You should have process manuals for all of the processes that are essential for your business, not just for training purposes but as part of your disaster recovery.

5. Reduce your availability.
    If you cannot resist offering advice and getting involved in the work that your team should be delivering, then try working in a different location a couple of days a week or arrange your meetings and calls when your team is working on that new project so that you won't be tempted to 'pop' in to check up.

When I first started devolving responsibilities to my team, I set earlier deadlines so that I had time to check work and send it back for changes if needed and sometimes if the timing was tight I'd make the changes needed on my teams laptops and send it from their machine to ensure that they owned the document and that the client was dealing directly with them.

Getting your team to take ownership is a two-way street. Whatever you do, try not to take over, give input where necessary and show appreciation for a job well done. Feeling appreciated is a big motivator, remember don't sweat the small stuff, if the outcome is what you needed the path isn't important.

CHAPTER FIVE

KNOWLEDGE SHARING

"If you have knowledge, let others light their candle in it"
— Margaret Fuller

To be a true leader, one who takes their business and team to astronomical growth, requires the ability to share knowledge freely and not be afraid of sharing what you've learnt on your journey so that others can have a faster trajectory than you have.

This however can be hard due to the fact that some of the lessons which have gotten us to where we are as business owners and leaders, were hard and painful.

When I first started attending networking events to build my network and promote my business, the moment another business owner announced that they were in the same space as me I would withdraw into my shell and the fear of sharing my knowledge reared it's head. I would literally give them the room full of potential clients! It took a while but I eventually realised that everyone has a USP (unique selling proposition) and my outlook and delivery will differentiate me and my business, it was not that I was inferior. It is possible that you have come across this path, the road of inferiority complex or what many call the 'imposter syndrome.'

Over time I found that sharing my knowledge in those forums helped to identify me to my ideal clients and listening to others helped me to decide if they were the type of client I would want to work with and know how best to form a proposal.

I often come across employees and business owners who are secretive about their work because they are afraid that if they tell someone all of their trade secrets they will no longer be required. Like Richard who was seconded to another department and didn't want to share his process manuals and templates with his team, because he felt that if he shared how he made his work easier someone else would take the credit or mess up the systems that he had put in place.

However, sharing our knowledge with our team and peers is key to finding the most effective methodologies and ensuring that customers receive a uniform service, this is especially needed when your teams work from different locations.

You want to ensure that wherever a customer encounters your business they have the same excellent experience. This only happens when knowledge sharing is standard across peer groups and a good way to make this happen is to create peer coaching groups so that your managers can share knowledge and challenges regularly and come to solutions as a collective.

My client David had two stores, the team working at one location was very structured and ordered but lacked creativity, the other team was more creative in their delivery, but could be disorganised. Both sets of clients were happy with the service that they were receiving but both were missing the excellence that would come from harnessing the best of both stores. I worked with David to provide tailored leadership training for his management team to make sure that they both had the process right and then I set up a peer coaching programme for the managers and deputy managers so that they could learn from each other. It made a big difference, the managers started collaborating on projects and asking each other for assistance instead of asking David, it led to greater client satisfaction and each location saw an increase in custom.

Collaborative working within your organisation will help your business to grow quickly and allow issues to be resolved at a fast pace, too often I have found that the answers that my clients are looking for can be found within their organisation. But they never ask.

One of my corporate clients wanted to recruit a more diverse workforce but were receiving applications from the same types of candidates. They reached out to specific agencies to seek out their ideal candidates but had limited success. We suggested that they change the imagery and language was being used on their adverts and advertised in region-specific media which worked well, however our suggestion of incentivising staff to recommend others worked the best. Your team will only recommend those that they believe will be successful in the role and excel within your business. Asking staff for recommendations should have been the first option and would have saved my client some time and money too.

Collaborative working within your organisation will help your business to grow

When I talk about sharing knowledge I don't just refer to what an individual needs to know to perform their role to the highest level. We also need to share knowledge about what is happening in our business and what is new in the marketplace with our team. Often businesses set sales and profitability targets at the beginning of the year but unless an individual is part of the senior or sales team they have no clue what is happening until something is announced in the news or the annual recruitment and training freeze happens in quarter four to ensure that the annual targets are achieved. This kind of behaviour can create uncertainty and fears of instability in your team and whenever staff are concerned about their role, they will start to look into the marketplace to see what roles are out there and if they are looking, they will find something.

It can be scary to let your team know that things aren't going as anticipated within your business, but your business savvy staff will have an inkling anyway. It is better to share your business progress and opportunities regularly and get input and ideas from your team so that they feel part of the business and they'll get used to the conversations as being a normal part of business life, rather than causes for concern. Whenever I've carried out a restructure or redundancy process there are always staff who say they knew something wasn't quite right and suggested great ideas for bringing increased revenue into the business or making savings, but by the time they are asked for input, it's too late to implement the suggestions.

At the end of last year I got involved in supporting a restructure and redundancy programme for the UK office of a US company, they had lost a major client in the autumn but had other projects in the pipeline and so hadn't spoken to staff to gather suggestions or look at ways to increase the efficiency of the business.

The projects in the pipeline were not confirmed and after months of making a loss, they announced a restructure with redundancies. The team had several ideas to increase revenue but they were all long term strategies that couldn't be actioned in time to save the roles, but the ideas may have saved roles if they were put in place in the autumn. This isn't an unusual case, we always hope for the best when life gets a little tricky but if one client can shake your business foundation, you should always be on the lookout for others and your team are best placed to identify those opportunities. Employer at times tend to overlook one of the most valuable asset to their business, their team and end up spending more time and money looking outside for answers when it was always there within the business.

How about having a quarterly blue sky thinking session with your team? Get the creative juices flowing. Decide on some pilots that your team can run with, it could be the beginning of something amazing.

Remember to regularly:

- Share your business objectives.
- Review team and individual objectives as the needs of the business change.
- Share your business wins and challenges.
- Ask for ideas to improve the business.
- Share your business ideas and ask for input.
- Don't be afraid to say "I don't know."

During your weekly or monthly team meetings, have each team or specialist individually host and share a bit about what they do and how the entire organisation can help them.

Also give opportunities for individuals to work in other areas of your business that are of interest to them, you may find out that they have some hidden skills.

Establishing a learning culture

It can be easy to forget to make time to focus on learning new skills or developing the ones that you have when you are busy running your business. There is barely time to keep all of the plates spinning! but we have to keep learning and ensure that our team is working to their best ability by building their skillset and empowering them to stretch and grow, even if it means that eventually, they will grow into a position outside of your business. Learning is an investment in both time and resources and when you are running a business there can be a fear that you will invest in building your team and they will take those skills and work elsewhere. However, we have to embrace the fact that no one will stay with your business forever – the average tenure for an employee is 4.6 years, so while you have them you should get the very best out of the team that you have. Plus staff who feel valued stick around longer, a survey from Investors in People (IIP) found that 33% of UK employees said they wanted to leave their job due to a lack of opportunity for career progression.

You need to build and nurture a learning culture so that sharing rather than hoarding knowledge becomes the norm. Learning and developing yourself and your team doesn't have to be expensive. It can be as simple as sharing your notes from a conference or an interesting article or sending one member of your team to an industry event and then asking them to present on their findings and any new ideas can work well too. Coaching and mentoring are great ways to build your team's knowledge and helping them to progress their careers.

What is the difference between coaching and mentoring you ask?

Coaching is generally task or objective related, helping an individual to do something specific and once that has been completed the relationship normally ends. Although it can last for an extended period, dependent on the objective.

To write this book I engaged with a book writing coach, once the book is complete our 1-2-1 coaching journey will end or pause until I start working on the next book in the Leading for Growth series!

Mentoring is generally long term and future focussed. They work best when the mentor isn't directly responsible for the mentee so that the mentees current role and responsibilities aren't shaping their future plans.

For example, I had a mentor who was an Operational IT Director, I was never going to be in the IT field so his advice on building my career wasn't dependent on my progress within his team or organisation; but he was able to give me insights, introduce me to concepts and people in his network who could help me to progress. It was really useful for me to develop my business awareness and to ask the difficult questions. To coach and mentor you need to understand the other persons, likes, dislikes, aspirations, hopes, fears and learning style. Then package your advice and instruction accordingly. You have to ask questions and then really listen and engage, then respond in an authentic way. It's pointless saying "I've been there" when you haven't. The idea is to use questions to help the other person come up with the solution, rather than just telling them. It takes time to build your skill at having this type of conversation without getting frustrated.

Good questions to ask include:

- What could the best outcome be?
- What part of what you just said could be an assumption?
- If I were in your shoes and asked you that question, what would you say?
- What are the positive outcomes of this negative situation?
- What would you try now if you knew you could not fail?
- When will you start?
- What are you waiting for?
- And?

Whether a person has a coach or mentor, it doesn't need to take them away from their work for a significant period of time. An hour a week in a coaching scenario or a couple of hours a month with a mentor can make all the difference.

Learning theory shows that the retention of training correlates to how we are taught. It is why I also include case studies and encourage role-play when I deliver training. We have to apply what we have learnt for it to stick.

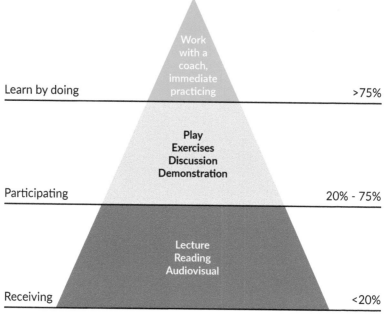

Retention of learning

At the moment I'm trying to develop a learning environment in my home with my daughters. It is a delicate balance, keeping learning fun but ensuring that they are where they are supposed to be developmentally, especially as I was brought up to study hard to achieve my goals and it didn't feel like fun! Don't get me wrong I got the job done but it felt like a chore at times and I really want to nurture my daughters' natural curiosity. One of the things that have helped me is knowing their learning style so that I can find the best way to get them to understand or retain information.

According to the VARK model, there are 4 primary types of learners; visual, auditory, reading/writing and kinaesthetic.

Visual learners learn best from visual representations such as, maps, spider diagrams, charts, graphs, flow charts, labelled diagrams, and all the symbolic arrows, circles, hierarchies and other elements, that can be used to represent what could have been presented in words. Auditory learners learn best by accessing information that is *"heard or spoken."* they learn best from lectures, group discussion, radio, using mobile phones, speaking, web-chat and talking things through. Reading/writing learners learn best from text-based input and output, reading and writing in all its forms but especially books, manuals, reports, essays and assignments. Kinaesthetic learners learn by getting hands-on and applying what they have learnt practically.

Most people have one or two ways in which they learn best, one of my daughters is read/write, the other one is kinaesthetic. It means what works with one child doesn't work with another, I have to change my style when teaching the same subject.

The same will apply to your team, don't make the mistake of thinking that one person is smarter than another just because they picked up a task quicker. We all learn differently. Find out how each of your team members learns best and use that when you are sharing information or training to ensure what you say sticks. Do not just rely on a PowerPoint; show videos, have discussions, do a case study, do role plays or a live demonstration on the system and get everyone to follow along on their laptops. Make the experience real.

CHAPTER SIX

EMOTIONAL RESILIENCE

"It isn't what we say or think that defines us, but what we do."
— *Jane Austen*

It's a tough life being an innovator, taking risks and daring to be different, the very definition of an entrepreneur is: *'A person who sets up business or businesses taking on financial risk in the hope of profit'* or *'One who organises, manages and assumes the risks of a business or enterprise'*. So, how do you build the mindset needed to be a risk-taker who bucks the trend and goes with their gut (with the right planning and research of course), so that when you face a challenge you can bounce back, repeatedly?

And the answer is RESILIENCE!

The definition of Resilience is *'the capacity to recover quickly from difficulties; toughness'*.

Resilience is all about how you deal with the challenges and obstacles that come your way. We all know that being an entrepreneur, leader or manager isn't all blue-sky thinking, ah-ha moments and sweet sales!

Not every idea will be a good one, not every client will love you and someone in your team will drive you to distraction as some point. The question is how will you bounce back when you feel stuck or get feedback that makes you question yourself?

A little while ago, as part of a training programme I told to ask friends, family, colleagues and clients for 3-5 words that they would use to honestly describe me and almost all of them said resilient as one of those words. I was surprised as I didn't write that down about myself, but as I thought about it I realised that I had been building my resilience all my life and love proving naysayers wrong. I loved it when I passed my driving test before my 'friend' who said they'd get theirs before me, or when I decided to go back to university to do my Masters and people told me it would be too hard as a newly-wed with a demanding full-time job. I've never let

Resilience is all about how you deal with the challenges and obstacles that come your way.

doubt or worry prevent me from going for what I really wanted!

*"Do not judge me by my success, judge me by how many times
I fell down and got back up again."*
— *Nelson Mandela*

Now while that worked for me in a personal capacity, I had to develop a different type of resilience when it came to leading others and building my business. I took things personally and saw any error as being down to a lack of skill on my part and a dent in my reputation. I was always hard on myself and possibly as you are reading this, you just might be saying in your mind, 'I am also guilty of doing the same.'

I hated submitting proposals and making sales calls because every no felt like I was being told that I was no good. The 'every no takes you closer to a yes' was totally lost on me. I was a person that didn't want to play the numbers game. Everything felt personal and so I had an emotional rather than a rational response. I was angry, frustrated and hurt that virtual strangers didn't see how much knowledge and value I would bring to their business. It made me ignore opportunities so that I avoided the possibility of rejection, which is no way to grow a business.

I vividly remember when a client of mine that I had a great working relationship with told me that they needed to terminate our contract because of cashflow. Then they didn't pay the final invoice and after a couple of months of chasing, I received notification that they had gone into receivership. I was crushed that my client didn't tell me how bad their financial issues were or ask for advice for releasing their staff correctly. I was upset and out of sorts for days.

My uncle who is an experienced business owner and my very first mentor told me that he'd been in my shoes and advised that I would probably never receive the payment and needed to write it off and move on. He shared a story about the time when he'd first started his business and he went and removed an item from a customer who kept promising to pay but never did. He said that he was so angry he didn't realise that he'd pulled a muscle in his back lifting the heavy equipment. It felt great at the time but he'd ended up in pain and still without the income.

"Do not judge me by my success, judge me by how many times I fell down and got back up again."

Nelson Mandela

I couldn't even imagine my uncle ever doing that he is the calmest, most pleasant individual I know, but everyone has their breaking point especially when it comes to their business baby.

YOU ARE MORE THAN YOUR BUSINESS OR ROLE

The fact is you are fabulous and you are striving to be better so that you can take your business to astronomical heights. You care enough about being a great leader and manager to invest time and money to read this book and implement the tips. You are adding to your skillset, which you'd only do if you cared. Caring is a prerequisite for anyone who leads people.

It took me a long time to separate my self-worth from my business and to realise that the perceived rejection of my business, wasn't a rejection of me, but once I got there I was able to deal with anything that was thrown at me and the business and find the lesson in the challenge. It also meant I was more graceful in accepting the 'No' which led to some becoming 'Yes' later on.

A person who is lacking in emotional resilience will find challenges and changes difficult to cope with and may display one or more of the following signs:

- Negative or depressed feeling
- Disappointment with themselves
- Increased emotional reactions - more tearful or sensitive or aggressive
- Loneliness, withdrawn
- Loss of motivation commitment and confidence
- Mood swings
- Confusion, indecision
- Difficulty concentrating
- Poor memory
- Changes in eating habits

- Increased smoking, drinking or drug-taking 'to cope'
- Mood swings affecting their behaviour
- Twitchy, nervous behaviour
- Changes in attendance such as arriving later or taking more time off

Look out for these signs in your team and yourself, get your team member to talk with someone; it could be you, a friend or their GP. Use the tips detailed in the **'Are you taking care of yourself'** section for dealing with stressors and refer to your occupational health service if you think it would be useful. You may also find that it would also be useful to have an assigned mental health first aider within your organisation, someone who can be on the lookout for signs of stress within your team and signpost the relevant support they need. Don't forget that your business has a duty of care to look after the mental health of the staff as part of your health and safety responsibilities.

Here are a few tips to help you remain focused and build your resilience:

Start your day right

I find that the tone with which I start my day has a big effect on my mood and productivity. I try to make sure that I start the day right by either going for a run or exercising most mornings. I also read a daily devotional and pray to set up my morning before the rest of my family wakes up. I find that exercising wakes my brain up and prayer puts my heart and mind in the right place.

Keep a Positive Attitude

I remember when I worked in customer services during my summer holidays, I realised that if angry customers shouted at me and I remained positive, I was able to calm them down, sort out their issue and not feel so stressed myself. It may sound corny but if you try to see the positive in every situation, there really is always a silver lining.

Don't take things personally

Your business is your 'baby', as an entrepreneur, it's difficult not to take things personally as you have put all your passion into achieving your dream and taken the associated risks. I used to get very emotional when things didn't turn out the way I planned, even when others gave me positive feedback, all I could see were the errors. You have to learn to separate your self-worth from the success of your business because everyone will have an opinion on your business but that doesn't mean it's how they think or feel about you. I've learnt to say "That's an interesting idea, thank you" and let it go.

Remember you can't please everyone

As a business owner, you try to please your clients or product users and keep your team motivated. It is good that this is your focus, however, remember that "You can please some of the people all of the time or all of the people some of the time". You can lose focus and begin to doubt yourself and doubt and fear have killed more dreams than failure. Therefore don't aim to be a people-pleaser but instead do what is right for your business, team and clients.

Take the comments at face value

It is easy to take what someone else says to heart and it doesn't take much for you to add your own interpretation or understanding, especially if it's shared online, as we can add emphasis at times where there is none. I know that I have been guilty of playing out a whole conversation in my head based on what I thought someone meant when they said something as opposed to what they actually said. My advice is to take the time to listen/read the comments and don't add your lens to it and that will help you to remain detached. Then take time to see if there is value in what had been shared.

Try these tips daily to build your resilience and you will feel more focussed and less stressed.

CHAPTER SEVEN

CURIOUSITY

"The important thing is not to stop questioning. Curiosity has its own reason for existing."
— *Albert Einstein*

What did you study? Where did you graduate? Where do you stay? Are you married?

I'd just started working with a new company and every meeting started this way. I felt like I was being interviewed all over again! But it was just their way of getting to know me – it was a quick way to establish some common ground.

And after a while I realised that it was perfectly fine to be curious, I found out things about individuals that would have taken me months in other companies because we English people can be a little too polite.

I was at a virtual networking event last week and the host asked us to introduce ourselves and say what our special power was and I said: "I'm nosy".

Now I'm not nosy just for the sake of it, I like to understand how things work and why things are done the way that they are done. Ask me to do something and nine times out of ten, I'll ask you a question to make sure that I truly understand what you want and why you need it, it's all about having clarity which I believe is very important to have when working with your clients, not that you are making your own assumption, suggestion yes but assumption no. Here's the thing, we don't know what we don't know, so if you tell me the background, I'll be better placed to give you the solution that you need. The same applies to when I communicate with my team, I could make assumptions about their knowledge and aspirations but it is better to ask the question and be sure.

I had a client who was grooming a member of her team to become her second in command and was crushed when he left to pursue a career in secondary education; she'd assumed that his insight and interest in her pre-school meant that he wanted to continue working with under 5's, but she hadn't asked, it meant that she'd wasted time and hadn't given the opportunity to others in her business that would have been more beneficial in the end. The good thing is that once she started asking the right questions of her team, she was able to identify those who wanted to progress and create a training plan for support them and this is a crucial element for the growth of your business and team. Before you start succession planning, have 1-2-1's with your team, you might get a surprise.

Some good questions to ask are:

- What do you enjoy about your role?
- What would you like to delegate?
- What is your ideal role?
- Where would you like to be in a year?
- What support do you need to achieve your aspirations?

You don't have to wait until it's performance time review for this to take place, constantly keeping up with your team's aspirations will help to avoid a lot of unwanted surprises.

How to ask the right questions

I'm an introvert which means that my natural inclination is to sit back and listen to what other people have to say. This is great for gathering information but I have to ask the right questions to get what I the answers needed and I can't just rely on the other people in the group to ask them for me. Generally, once I tell people what I do, they'll have a story to tell me about a tricky employee or a manager that they didn't like, while that is great, I need to take it to the next level to find out what their current problem or opportunity is and how I might be able to help them.

When it comes to my team or my client's teams, I have to be strategic about my questioning, especially if I have a course of action in mind.

A pre-school governance board engaged me to refresh their contract and policies, and while everything needed updating, they really wanted to me to help them to implement robust sickness absence and time-keeping policies so that they could actively address any issues.

Deeper questioning from me meant that I was able to identify exactly what they needed, yes they needed the policies but more than that a mechanism for recording and monitoring sickness and lateness was also necessary as they were not always in the building during the preschool hours. Issuing new contracts and an employee handbook would not have been enough, I needed to make sure that they were able to follow through on the policies that I was giving them, if I hadn't asked the right questions I would have missed a vital part of their solution and while they'd have shiny policies they wouldn't have been able to gather the evidence they needed to identify and address persistent lateness or patterns of sickness absence.

Being curious (or nosy) doesn't mean Interrogating a person, you just have to ask the right questions:

- Ask open questions

This gives the person(s) and the opportunity to fully articulate themselves and take the conversation in the direction that most appeals to them.

- Actively listen
Spend your time absorbing what they are saying and not saying.

- Watch out for non-verbal clues
Look out for body language and interactions with others, if you are speaking with a group.

- Don't make assumptions
Go into the conversation with an open mind, if you think you know the answer you will direct the questions to get to the answer you need.

Being curious (or nosy) doesn't mean Interrogating a person, you just have to ask the right questions

- Clarify any points that aren't clear
There is no such thing as a silly question, probe a point until you have an answer that you are clear about.

- Share your thought processes
Share what you've learnt and the actions that you think are appropriate and continue to get feedback regularly.

This will work whether you are making a plan with your team, engaging a service provider, signing up a new client or taking care of an existing client.

Be curious, people like to talk about themselves. Everybody likes to feel important, seen and understood; these elements are key for connecting with others. I've never met a person that I didn't have something in common with and finding a connection will open up all kinds of possibilities.

COURAGE

"Courage is the most important of all the virtues because without courage, you can't practice any other virtue consistently."

— *Maya Angelou*

When I started my business I knew who I wanted to serve and what I wanted to do, but I was constantly swayed by the opinions of others. This as you can imagine was frustrating because it then meant that I kept changing or caused myself unnecessary delay.

I was told not to do both HR and Career Coaching – I do both now!

I was told to offer services outside of my specialities for my clients – I don't do that any more, I know my zone of genius! This is an area where some business owners miss it, wanting to run a one-size fits all business and sell services

> *"Courage is the most important of all the virtues because without courage, you can't practice any other virtue consistently."*
>
> *Maya Angelou*

that they cannot provide for their clients. This can lose you your business as well as your position as an expert in your field. Whether you are running a business and/or managing a team you need to have the courage of your convictions, this means that you have to own your decisions and stand in your truth, even if it is unpopular or risky. You have to be clear about what you stand for, because staying silent or not taking action when something goes against your values, is saying something.

There was a story in the press last year about a police officer in the US who was captured on video at the scene of a verbal assault doing NOTHING – he didn't say anything, didn't attempt to intervene, he just stood at a distance watching, even though the person being assaulted asked the officer for help. Then following the backlash we were told that he had resigned.

Now obviously a police officer not serving and protecting is an issue, but any employee or contractor who isn't delivering as expected is an issue too! And if you do nothing, nothing will change.

When it comes to staff issues often no action is taken because…well because it's not the priority.

"If you truly prioritise something, you will make time for it."

Clients often come to us with issues that started weeks or months before and were not addressed as there were other more pressing priorities. However, the problem with not addressing staff issues is that they very rarely disappear. They escalate instead and take more time and resource to resolve.

HR Policies contain timelines for a reason, it is to ensure that issues are dealt with in a timely manner. If too long has passed since an incident occurred, you can't take action or use it as evidence.

Jane came to me regarding an employee who was turning up to work late on a regular basis. She wanted to terminate their employment as this had been going on for months. I asked to see the notes from meetings and any disciplinary outcomes that had been given and I was told that nothing officially documented and any conversations had been informal. I couldn't help Jane to exit that employee, it was far too risky. Instead, we had to start the disciplinary process to inform and address the lateness issue. In the end, after being given a written warning, the employee turned around their performance and is now working well.

"If you truly prioritise something, you will make time for it."

I must admit that not everyone is as lucky, had the employee's timekeeping not improved, it would have taken between 4-6 weeks at a minimum before she could have safely been exited from the business.

To ensure that you don't end up in the same position as Jane remember to:

- Address issues as they occur
  As soon as you can have a private conversation do so and follow it up with an email (and formal meeting request if that is necessary).

- Gather all the evidence while it is fresh
  Get any witnesses to write down what happened, check CCTV or IT records. Most systems don't keep things for a long period.

- Document everything
  Any meetings or conversations should be followed up with an email. Make sure you keep a timeline of events to help you keep track.

- Follow the process as detailed in your policies
  To ensure that you are covered should an employee take further action, make sure you can demonstrate that you have followed the guidelines set out in your relevant policies and procedures documents.

This morning I was showing my husband some new abs exercises and he was saying that he was finding some of the moves challenging (I was sharing the torture I have to endure at my boot-camp class!), when my amazing five-year old put her hand on his shoulder, looked him deep in the eyes and said "Daddy, you just need to keep practising and you'll get better".

We laughed because she sounded like me at homework time! I try to make homework fun and give feedback that builds my girls confidence and encourages them to keep pushing for excellence.

This can be very similar to dealing with staff issues, it can be hard to balance providing constructive feedback that motivates, rather than frustrates. And of course everyone is different, which means you need to flex your style of delivery to ensure that your word will be heard as intended. Do not be rigid as the approach needed to be taken with your team varies based on the individuals as opposed to the team on a whole.

It's always best to address issues as they occur (or as soon as you are aware), rather than storing them up for the next scheduled meeting or performance review. I always say that if someone is overachieving or underachieving they should know about it before going into a formal meeting or appraisal.

We all know that no one is perfect and we all make mistakes, so expecting perfectionism from your team is unrealistic. However, there are basics that need to be delivered, and processes and procedures that need to be adhered to.

The first step in dealing with staff issues is to ensure that they are aware of what is expected of them through establishing SMART (Specific, Measurable, Achievable, Realistic, Timely) objectives and having an employee handbook that details policies and procedures, around behaviour and the sanctions for not adhering to them.

Does your team have SMART objectives set? If you need a reminder on setting objectives, check out my video here: **https://youtu.be/OojcB63lVy8**

Does your team know what is expected of them? And how their work relates to the success of your business?

It is important to get confirmation from your team that they have heard and understood what you told them, I generally get my team to send me their objectives after we have discussed them, so that I can be sure they have understood what I relayed and not made any assumptions. Once you know that you and your team are on the same page, you are in a much better situation when it comes to dealing with any performance issues that arise.

Here are some tips to help you to discuss poor performance:

- Listen before you speak
  Get the back story, make sure there are no extenuating circumstances. Remember that sometimes your team needs your support more than your wrath!

- Be prepared
  Provide examples of issues and demonstrate what good looks like.

- Don't get emotional
  The majority of the time people aren't purposely making mistakes, they will feel bad, don't make it worse by adding your feelings to it.

- Be prepared to take a break
  If the conversation gets heated you can adjourn, reschedule or arrange for support (HR or a colleague) to be present.

- Explain the next steps
  Dependent on the issue, it could be training, a progress review in a few days, a performance improvement plan or disciplinary investigation

CHAPTER NINE

TRANSPARENCY

"Don't expect loyalty when you can't provide honesty"
— *Unknown*

"Open", "Honest" and "Transparent" are words that a lot of organisations use when it comes to their values. One of the things that I've found over the years is that this value isn't actively demonstrated throughout the business. There is a tendency to tell our team and our customers what we believe they want to hear, rather than being upfront and open regardless of the outcome.

In order to build your business and develop a team that will take your business to the next level and beyond you need to be open. I remember interviewing for role with a multi-million turnover organisation who when I asked some direct questions revealed to me that they had one major client, a huge food retailer that pretty bankrolled the majority of the business and so the whole business was structured to service this client and all the other smaller clients basically got the sloppy seconds.

Now if they lost that client the business would not have been sustainable and they were not being particularly proactive in looking for additional clients. I decided not to join and took an alternative offer – it was too risky for me at that time and there were a few other things that concerned me. A few years later, that company no longer existed.

I needed that information so that I could make an informed decision about that job offer. That ability to make an informed decision or give valuable input is the thing that we take away from our team and clients when we aren't open and sharing the full picture. I can decide for myself and my family on starting a business or taking a role where funding has only been secured for the next six months based on where I am in life and what income I need, but if you don't tell me what's happening and I think I'm taking a secure position only to find out in six months that I cannot pay my mortgage, I would be

In order to build your business and develop a team that will take your business to the next level and beyond you need to be open

justified to be upset because I wasn't aware of all of the detail and therefore couldn't make an informed choice.

This type of behaviour breaks trust and trust once broken is extremely hard to rebuild.

"Trust is lost in buckets and earned back in drops"
— Michael Todd

Being open and honest isn't just about what you share with your team, it's also about what you don't share. Lying by omission is still lying.

I remember starting a redundancy consultation, fully aware that as soon as it was complete another one would start in the next department and then the next. Although I knew it would be virtually impossible for the unions to keep the whole programme a secret, I chose to lay all our cards on the table and share the full extent of our savings target at once. It meant having all of my service heads in a room with the unions for a few hours but at the end of it, we were able to achieve our target with less drama. Being open and transparent is really a value that you need to take time to delve into and visibly demonstrate to your team and clients. You need to make sure your team are aware of, the importance of that transparency and honesty cannot be underestimated, so if you know that there is a mistake, issue or challenge let them know. If there is a concern or worry share it, because they may already be worrying about that same thing and it's much better if you let them know because it builds a much better relationship and trust.

In my house we have a deal, if you tell the truth you won't get punished. So my girls know that they have two opportunities (sometimes three) to tell the truth when we asked them what happened and if later on, we find out differently (or we'd heard it ourselves) they will be punished. They will always have to apologise and rectify the mistake if possible but they know that there isn't going to be a punishment, they aren't going to be without a toy or lose their tablet privileges. We are striving to teach them honesty over everything else and it's hard because sometimes you don't want to hear the truth and sometimes it hurts, but it's important because when things go wrong, as they always will do when it comes to running a business; you want your team to be comfortable enough to tell you that there's a problem.

"Trust is lost in buckets and earned back in drops"

Michael Todd

I remember working on some bid calculations looking at the redundancy figures and things I had completed before I went on maternity leave but the timings had changed. Therefore, I reviewed it all and said they were fine but a couple of days later, I went back into the spreadsheet to review something else and realised that the dates were incorrect, which meant that some of the redundancy figures were lower than they ought to be.

I went straight back to my boss and said "I'm really sorry, I don't know how I missed this", I could have said nothing and hoped no one would notice but that wasn't professional and it was early enough to fix it. There may be things that you delay to disclose and it in the end makes matters worse, you may just run into exactly what you were trying to avoid.

So practically there are two things that you need to do about the honest and transparency stuff.

The first thing is to be yourself, if you've had a bad day or you've made a mistake or you've been chewed out by a customer - share it - don't pretend everything is fine. Let your team know what you've done to improve or rectify things so that they can see what good looks like and emulate your swan-like composure.

Let your team know that you have a life that sometimes gets priority over the business and that you'll be understanding when the same thing happens in their life. You have to set the example. I was listening to Michelle Obama's podcast when she interviewed one of her first bosses, she explained that her boss always took calls from her daughter irrespective of what meeting she was in and that watching her boss switch from commanding a meeting to being a mummy and back again, gave her the courage to set clear boundaries for her work and family time even when she was the first lady. Sometimes your team needs to see the possibilities to know that you can demand them.

My team know that I don't take calls until I've taken my children to school. I want to give them my full attention because I can get loads of valuable information on that walk. So if I call a member of my team and I can hear their child in the background I'll always ask if they want to talk later. I don't want them to hide the fact that they have children at home the way that I did when I first started my business. I used to go out in the garden so that my clients couldn't hear them.

Secondly, you have to call out any things that could be viewed as not being upfront. One of the classic examples is of people ignoring calls from people that they'd rather not talk to, it's only delaying the inevitable or moving the problem to someone else in the team. If you see this type of behaviour be clear that it isn't acceptable.

Show that the rules apply to everyone, you aren't exempt. Don't put a private meeting in your diary that's really your mani/pedi, call it what it is. Your team know that you work uber hard and hardly ever have a lunch break, two hours out of the office is more than due.

Treat your team like adults unless there is a reason why they need to be sat at their desks at 9 am sharp, don't make timekeeping the issue. Focus on the job getting completed to a high standard, one time and on budget.

If you are running late, let your team know and be honest about the reason (unless it's private and/or confidential) and let them know you expect the same. No sneaking in trying to act as if you were always there.

Everybody makes mistakes but they won't openly admit that to their boss if they feel like they're going to get punished for being human and after all that's what you're doing punishing them for being human.

I do believe that when we are open and transparent with our staff, they will be the same with our customers. Your customers will appreciate it if you can say this is what went wrong and this is how we're going to fix it. We are really sorry that you've had this experience and we are going to work hard to make sure that this doesn't happen again; rather than trying to apportion blame and not taking full ownership of it.

Growing your business is really about is taking ownership and giving ownership or responsibility to others to ensure that you are free to focus on the things that you need to do. You need to trust those you are delegating to and building that relationship requires openness.

Change is hard, but I've learnt through years of supporting others through change, that there are a few things you need to help it go smoothly:

Detail the Rationale

Be clear about why the change is necessary. Don't be afraid to share the details and why it will benefit the business, try to answer the questions your team will have before they ask.

Detail the steps

Have a clear plan, with steps for part of your change project. Show the timelines and where dependencies and pinch points may be. You need your team to understand what will be needed from them.

Celebrate each milestone

Don't wait until the end to celebrate, each achievement is worth celebrating and having some fun will energise you for the next step

Take a break

Change can be all-consuming, it's good to do some tasks that are unrelated to it. Also, taking time to step away, can give you more perspective.

Try these tips and growing pain won't be such a pain.

CHAPTER TEN

CLEAR COMMUNICATOR

"Communicate unto the other person that which you would want him to communicate unto you if your positions were reversed."
— Aaron Goldman

My company communicates with me too much, said no employee ever!

Well that's not strictly true!

I worked for a large consultancy who sent out all their staff communications by email, between the HR, IT, Recruitment, Marketing and unit specific communications staff could receive several emails a day. So, the staff got email fatigue and stopped reading them. I'd have my monthly team meeting and start talking about a new initiative and no one would have heard of it, some of my team told me that they had set up a rule to automatically file the emails in a folder and they never got around to looking at it. This meant that I had to go out of my way to ensure that my team and those on my account were hearing the information I needed them to hear.

I found three things that worked much better than the email; a quick 5-minute scrum first thing in the morning, a lunchtime meeting where I'd bring in some tasty deserts and we could eat and chat or physical copies of the staff newsletter, left in the common areas of the building.

You see when you communicate there are two things that need to happen:

One – You transmit your message.

Two – Your message is received as transmitted.

You could have the most amazing message or opportunity to share but if no one is receiving what you are transmitting, you may as well save your breath or fingers. You need to check that what you have communicated has been received, miscommunication is often the reason why targets get missed or a task isn't completed in the way that you expected.

It is important not to just put the information out there but to check that your team has understood it. During my 5 minute morning scrum I'd get everyone to tell me about their priority for the day, I could easily change their priority or give some insight to help the process. The lunchtime sessions, was a chance to have a discussion, make suggestions and ask questions. I often got more from those sessions than a formal team meeting as there wasn't an agenda, just a subject to be discussed.

Do you find it a challenge to get a straight answer from your team?

Ever had a client ask you what's happening or tell you about a problem that you were not aware of?

Are you trying not to micromanage your team, but you aren't getting the updates that you need?

Back then I was working corporately, I was often away from my office working on tenders and I struggled to stay updated with what was happening with my team back in head office. Beyond our regularly scheduled catch-ups, I'd need to call or corner someone in the break room to get caught up. I found it stressful as I was often only in the office for client meetings and would pitch up with a report to present but not have the background to deal with any issues or concerns. It was my fault I didn't set out my expectations correctly, I agreed objectives with my team and didn't tell them that I needed regular check-ins or ask for the narrative behind the reports.

Trusting your team to deliver and keep you updated with what's happening, shouldn't be a challenge but it can be hard to find the balance between giving your team the freedom to deliver and micromanaging.

You want your team to be problem solvers, not problem multipliers and work within their zone of genius, but if you don't ask for what you need from your team, the problem with their performance might not be them, it might be you.

Working with teams based in different locations, working a variety of shifts and on multiple projects would be difficult to juggle for anyone.

Here are 5 things you can implement to help you stay on top of what's happening:

Daily/weekly team briefings

A half an hour meeting at the start or the end of the day to discuss priorities and any challenges will give you comfort that your team are on the right track, or if they are not will allow you to redirect their attention.

Weekly online updates

Create a template that is updated weekly in your file share (google docs, dropbox, etc). I like the OKR (Objectives and Key Results) method as an easy way to check progress on objectives – find out more here https://www.edenmayers.com/blog/got-a-pen

Be specific about what you need

Schedule a regular call for when that report drops or client meeting is due, so that you can discuss it in-depth or be clear about when your team needs to give you a heads up that a client has a problem, even though they are on top of it.

Shadow and delegate

Provide opportunities for your team to shadow your interactions and present the reports so that they can see the purpose of their objective and get a deeper understanding of your client's expectations.

Add a buffer

Don't leave things to the last minute, give yourself some time to review and reflect by setting a deadline that's at least 24 hours before the item is needed, this also gives you time to ask for amendments rather than doing them yourself.

In any relationship, business or personal communication is the key. You could cover everything that is detailed in this book with the umbrella of communication.

Great communication opens the door to everything because that is where understanding comes from. Nothing is more frustrating than having a conversation, delivering a presentation or training and finding that no one understood what you were saying.

No one like to feel that they have communicated and it's fallen into a void, so timely responding is vital. Often I've sent a message to someone to check days later and see it hasn't been read.

One of the things that I share with my teams and friends alike is that the best way to connect with me is by text, it will pop up on my Apple Watch or the screen of my info-centre when I'm driving and as soon as I'm able I'll respond. I spend my days in meetings and on calls, so voicemails may not be picked up for a while and emails can get lost in the pile.

Do your team know the best way to get hold of you? And do you know the best way to get hold of them?

Next time you meet with your team, ask them how they like to be communicated with, knowing that if you send an email you should follow up with a text could be the making of a wonderful relationship.

I worked with a manager who would say, "just because you've emailed me doesn't mean that I've taken action, come and speak to me or call."

In today's fast-paced world we sometimes forget about the personal touch, we are all individuals who want to feel heard. Take the time to let your team know that you've heard and understood them.

CHAPTER ELEVEN

THE ROUND-UP

I mentioned earlier about being completely open and honest, I want to do exactly that right now by admitting to you that I really don't know how to end this book, because I have so much more that I have to share but I am aware that to give you all this book would never end.

I have given you some tips for leading yourself effectively and the values and behaviours that you want to look for and develop in your team and yourself to really be an effective leader as you grow and scale your business. I want to tell more about how to manage and motivate your team, stay legislatively compliant but still be your authentic self so that you avoid employee issues escalating and should they escalate you will be about to demonstrate that you have followed policy and process.

Originally this book had a third practical HR section on policies but I made the decision to write another book so that I could get these nuggets to you faster, giving you the opportunity to start implementing straightaway, as once you've nailed your leadership and management style and behaviours, all the other elements will be fall into place a lot easier. So watch out for part two in 2021.

Right now I want you to take this book and use it to help you to become the most effective leader you can possibly be; to coach and mentor your team to be the very best that they can be, whether they are already leading a team or are aspiring to lead a team so that they won't just be great at doing their job but also at will be great leaders and managers of people. And understand the difference; how to lead so that they motivate and take their team with them on their journey and how to manage well to ensure that the day to day is happening, that the tasks are being completed to a high standard within the agreed timelines, that work is continuously improving, that customers are happy. That your team are happy, learning and stretched so that they are working to their full potential so that your team are getting the satisfaction of a job well done and you are able to concentrate on doing what you do best and having the work-life balance you desire

That is my wish for you and your team as you build your business

I would love to hear your key takeaways, what things you improved, changed or implemented in both the way you lead yourself and others and any aha moments, do contact me at info@edenmayers.com

If you need any support with your leadership, management or HR strategy for your teams schedule a FREE call with us https://www.edenmayers.com/teamstrategycall

HAPPY LEADING!

ABOUT THE AUTHOR

Melanie Folkes-Mayers is a multi-award winning entrepreneur, human resources professional, career coach, speaker, teacher and first-timer author.

With a Masters in Human Resources Management and Chartered MCIPD qualified, she also has a Prince 2 Project Management Qualification.

Melanie has honed her craft working with businesses from small to multinational, in industries including; IT, Retail, Publishing and Consulting. Melanie has never shied away from a challenge, and so her career trajectory skyrocketed as she filled a Head of HR role in her early thirties.

Melanie found that as much as she enjoyed leading a large multidisciplinary team, she also wanted to keep getting involved in the nitty-gritty HR work and moved into working on mergers and acquisitions, loving getting to know varying organisations, formulating HR solutions and working on projects with leaders and managers to ensure staff moved seamlessly from one organisation to another.

As Melanie's career developed she found herself providing HR and career advice to friends and associates more and more frequently. More than once she was advised to start her own HR consultancy, and in February 2014 when her first child turned one-year-old, Eden Mayers Limited was incorporated and named after her daughter; by February 2015 Melanie was the mother of two active girls and started the process of turning her side hustle into a full-time gig.

"I wanted the challenge of interesting work and supporting clients to be excellent leaders and managers, but didn't want to miss my girls growing up. I needed to be able to control when and where I worked, it wasn't a big ask but I wasn't able to find that corporately without being put on the mummy track"

In July 2016 Melanie took the plunge to leave the corporate world and work full-time as CEO of Eden Mayers HR Consulting, working mainly with clients in London and the South East, but providing HR support as far afield as Barbados and South Africa.

Melanie's great passion is building great leaders who manage their teams with integrity, *"Leading your team proactively, addressing issues when they occur, taking that extra time to plan for your people, really taking their ideas and thoughts in mind and communicating clearly and transparently can prevent a lot of drama"*

When Melanie is not keeping her clients out of HR trouble, she loves to cook and bake with her girls, get lost in a good book, run competitive races and explore the world with her family.

GREAT LEADERS
By Meiji Stewart

Awaken minds.
Bring people together.
Communicate effectively.
Dare to take calculated risk.
Enlighten and empower.
Foster collaboration.
Give you tools to succeed.
Help you do for yourself.
Invite and encourage questions.
Joyfully embrace diversity.
Keep an open mind.
Lead by example.
Motivate with respect.
Never give up on you.
Open doors to new worlds.
Put first things first.
Quest to make learning fun.
Recognize problems early.
Share roles and responsibilities.
Take time to explain issues.
Unwrap talents and abilities.
Values everyone's inputs.

Welcome mistakes as part of learning.
Exceeds expectations.
Yen to connect, not correct.
Zest to make a difference.

ACKNOWLEDGEMENTS

Firstly, I have to give thanks to God for inspiring me to write this book and putting all the things in place that I needed to complete it.

Love and thanks to my amazing husband Daniel and my daughters Eden and Zahara, for supporting my work and sacrificing time with me while I pursued this dream – there is a big holiday on the horizon!

To my spiritual sister Grace, always there with an encouraging word and practical support – My success is your success.

Finally to my amazing coaches, Naomi Aidoo, Janine Cummings, Michelle Watson. Each of you has given me the skills, knowledge and support to get this book done and take my business to the next level – I'm forever grateful.

BIBLIOGRAPHY

The Big Leap – Gay Hendricks

The Best Yes – Lysa TerKeurst

Mental Health First Aid (MHFA) England

PHOTO CREDIT

Penny Dampier